Abby Langdon Alger

The Little Flowers of Saint Francis of Assisi

Vol. 1

Abby Langdon Alger

The Little Flowers of Saint Francis of Assisi
Vol. 1

ISBN/EAN: 9783337342876

Printed in Europe, USA, Canada, Australia, Japan

Cover: Foto ©Lupo / pixelio.de

More available books at **www.hansebooks.com**

The Little Flowers

OF

Saint Francis of Affifi.

In the Name of Our Lord and Saviour
JESUS CHRIST, who was crucified, and of His
Mother the VIRGIN MARY. In this Book
are contained certain Little Flowers, Miracles,
and devout Examples of that glorious poor
Follower of Chrift, Saint Francis, and
of certain of his holy Companions.
Told to the Praife of Jefus
Chrift. Amen.

Translated from the Italian,

With a Brief Account of the Life of Saint Francis,

By ABBY LANGDON ALGER.

BOSTON:
LITTLE, BROWN, AND COMPANY.
1898.

PREFACE.

SAINT FRANCIS was born in 1182, in the little town of Affifi, in Umbria, chiefly notable as having given him birth. His mother, Madonna Pica, was of noble race, and his father, Peter Bernardone, that is, Peter the fon of Bernard, the family name being Moriconi,—was a rich merchant, who was travelling in France on bufinefs at the time Francis was born. Many ftrange tales are told of the omens attending the little boy's advent into the world. For fome time previous, a poor man roamed the ftreets of Affifi crying aloud, "Peace and profperity! peace and profperity!" His mother was ill for many days, nor were her fufferings relieved, until by the advice of a pilgrim who came that way ſhe was laid on a bed of ſtraw in a ſtable. Thus began that likeneſs between the life of Francis and that of Chriſt, which was continued throughout.) Another ſtranger appeared to act as godfather, and ſtill another took the baby in his arms and, marking his right ſhoulder with a croſs, foretold the victory which he was to win over the Devil. Madonna Pica named her child John, in memory of the beloved diſciple; but on his father's return with rich profits, he choſe to call him Francis, for the country where he had been ſo ſucceſsful.

The boy was taught by the prieſts of the pariſh, and learned eaſily all that was taught him, ſhowing an eſpecial talent for the language of the land from which he took his name. As he grew to manhood he was foremoſt in the gayeties of the town, winning for himſelf the ſobriquet of the "flower of youth."

Thomas of Celano, a Franciſcan

brother, and a dear friend of Francis, describes him thus: "He was of middle stature, rather under than over, with an oval face and full but low forehead, his eyes dark and clear, his hair thick, his eyebrows close, a straight and delicate nose, a voice soft yet keen and fiery; close, equal, and white teeth; lips modest yet subtle; a black beard not thickly grown; a thin neck, square shoulders, short arms, small hands and feet, delicate skin, and little flesh." So elegant was his dress, and so luxurious were his tastes, that his parents often said, "He is more like the son of a prince than like our son." Still, they were proud of his splendor, and grudged him nothing, though his charities were as lavish as his pleasures: no beggar ever asked of him in vain.

When he had reached the age of twenty-four, however, a war broke out between Assisi and Perugia. Francis was taken prisoner, and for a year languished in captivity. Returning home, he suffered from a long and tedious illness which proved a turning-point in his career. He began to long for something better and higher than mere amusement. It was the age of knighthood, and his first thought was to redress wrong and help the weak. He set out to join the forces of the Count de Brienne, described as a man of great magnificence and liberality; but stopping at Spoleto, he was warned in a dream to return home, which he did in a state of melancholy and absorption. His merry comrades laughingly asked if he was dreaming of a wife, that he was so sober. "Yes," was the answer,— "of a wife more noble, more beautiful, and more rich than anything your fancy can conceive." This bride was Poverty, whom he was so soon to espouse. He now began to devote himself more entirely to the sick and poor, particularly the lepers, of whom there were many at that time. These wretched beings were shunned by

Preface.

every one, and Francis muſt indeed have ſeemed mad to thoſe who ſaw him ſtoop to kiſs their infectious forms.

Going one day to the ruined Church of St. Damian's, an inward voice bade him repair it. At once he hurried home, and his father being away, took a quantity of merchandiſe, which he ſold, offering the price for the work of reſtoration. The prieſt refuſing, he threw it in a corner, where it lay until the angry Peter Bernardone, learning what had happened, came to claim it and to impriſon his headſtrong ſon. His mother finally freeing him, he ſought refuge with the prieſt of St. Damian's, reſtoring to his father all that he had received from him, even his clothes, ſtripping himſelf to the hair ſhirt which he had worn in ſecret, and renouncing his father forever. Thenceforth he begged material to repair the church from door to door, building it up with his own hands, and collecting broken ſcraps of food from the charitable, for his maintenance. In this way, in the courſe of two years he reſtored three churches and gained twelve diſciples, the firſt being Bernard of Quintavalle. The ſtory of their converſion and final formation into the Order of Friars Minor, Gray Friars, or Franciſcan Monks, is told in the "Little Flowers" which follow. Within eleven years theſe twelve grew to more than five thouſand. They were vowed to abject poverty, owning abſolutely nothing, thus differing from the other eccleſiaſtical bodies then in exiſtence.

Francis next founded the Order of Poor Ladies, afterwards known as the Poor Clares, in honor of their firſt abbeſs, Clara Sciffi, a beautiful heireſs, who left her home at the age of fifteen to enter upon a religious life. Later ſtill the third Order was eſtabliſhed, which was open to men and women alike, and meant for thoſe who lived in the world. Theſe three Orders ſpread rapidly throughout the globe,

Saint Francis travelling even into Syria.

After enduring every privation and sorrow for many years, as well as many namelefs raptures in his spiritual intercourfe with God, he faw, as he prayed upon a lonely mountain, a vifion of Chrift crucified; and as he gazed, his body became ftamped with the Stigmata, or marks of the Paffion of our Lord, which he thenceforth bore until his death, fome two years after, Oct. 4, 1226, in the forty-fifth year of his age.

The chief quality of Saint Francis — the central and charaCteriftic charm which has made him perhaps the beft beloved of all the illuftrious members of the calendar — is the depth and tendernefs of his heart. His gentle and generous affeCtion was conftantly overflowing on all around him, in fympathetic attention, poetic expreffions, and aCts of endearment. The objeCts of his intenfe and exuberant love were not only God, angels, and men, but also animals, birds, insects, and even inanimate objects, which he was wont to address as his brothers and sisters, in reference to their common origin with himself. Many charming instances of his friendships with fish, falcons, swallows, lambs, wolves, hares, pheasants, and grasshoppers, may be found in these "Little Flowers," and in the various Lives of him.

He was first to establish the custom still prevalent in Catholic countries, of representing the Nativity in the stable at Bethlehem, at Christmas time, before the altar. He was also among the earliest of Italian poets; for in those days Italian was only the vulgar tongue, Latin or the soft Provençal being used for literary purposes. He improvised many ardent hymns and songs, which he taught to his followers, the most widely known being the "Canticle to the Sun," or "Song of the Creatures," and "Love sets my Heart on Fire."

Preface.

Many full and interesting Lives of Saint Francis have been written in various tongues, the best being those by Thomas of Celano and by Saint Bonaventura, — his friends and disciples, — by Father Luke Wadding, by Mrs. Oliphant, by M. Chavin de Malin, and by a Religious of the Order of Poor Clares. The "Little Flowers" are a series of legends which were collected some two hundred years after his death, having been handed down by word of mouth until that time. They form an excellent biography of him and his disciples, told with quaint simplicity and grace. The translator has tried to preserve the *naïveté* and antique flavor of the original in the present version. The work being so famous and favorite a classic in Italy and France, it is somewhat singular that it has never until now been presented in English.

A. L. A.

November, 1887.

CONTENTS.

CHAPTER I.

PAGE

In the Name of Our Lord and Saviour Jefus Chrift, Who was crucified, and of His Mother the Virgin Mary. In this Book are contained certain Little Flowers, Miracles, and Devout Examples of that glorious poor Follower of Chrift, Saint Francis, and of certain of his holy Companions. Told to the Praife of Jefus Chrift. Amen . . . 7

CHAPTER II.

Of Brother Bernard of Quintavalle, the firft Companion of Saint Francis 9

CHAPTER III.

How for the evil Thoughts which Saint Francis had regarding Brother Bernard, he commanded that fame Brother Bernard that three Times he fhould place his Feet upon his Neck and upon his Mouth 16

CHAPTER IV.

How the Angel of the Lord put a Queſtion unto Brother Elias, the Keeper of a certain Convent in the Vale of Spoleto, and foraſmuch as Brother Elias made Anſwer haughtily, departed thence and went forth unto St. James of Compoſtella, where he met with Brother Bernard and told his Tale unto him 21

CHAPTER V.

How that Saint, Brother Bernard of Aſſiſi, was deſpatched by Saint Francis to Bologna, and there took up his abode . . . 29

CHAPTER VI.

How Saint Francis bleſſed Brother Bernard and made him his Vicar when he came to paſs away from this Life 33

CHAPTER VII.

How Saint Francis faſted forty Days and forty Nights in an Iſland of the Lake of Perugia, eating no more but half a Loaf 37

CHAPTER VIII.

How Saint Francis and Brother Leo, as they journeyed, diſcourſed of Perfect Bliſs . . 40

CHAPTER IX.

How Saint Francis taught Brother Leo to make Anſwer unto Him; and He could never Speak ſave the Contrary of that which Saint Francis Willed 44

CHAPTER X.

How Brother Maximus Mockingly ſaid unto Saint Francis that the World was at his Feet, and he made Anſwer that this was by the Grace of God, and a Diſgrace to the World 48

CHAPTER XI.

How Saint Francis cauſed Brother Maximus to turn himſelf about, and then departed unto Sienna 50

CHAPTER XII.

How Saint Francis beſtowed on Brother Maximus the offices of Gate-Keeper, Almoner, and Cook: then at the Prayer of the other Brothers deprived him of them 55

CHAPTER XIII.

How Saint Francis and Brother Maximus laid the Bread which they had begged upon a Stone beſide a Well, and Saint Francis loudly praiſed Poverty. Then he prayed

unto God and Saint Peter and Saint Paul
that they might enamour Him of divine
Poverty; and how Saint Peter and Saint
Paul appeared unto Him 58

CHAPTER XIV.

How Saint Francis, difcourfing of God with
his Brethren, He appeared in their Midft . 64

CHAPTER XV.

How Saint Clara ate with Saint Francis and
with his Brother Monks in St. Mary of
the Angels 65

CHAPTER XVI.

How Saint Francis received the Advice of
Saint Clara and of Holy Brother Sylvefter,
that he fhould go forth and preach, converting the People; and he created the
Third Order, and preached to the Birds
and filenced the young Swallows . . . 69

CHAPTER XVII.

How a Francifcan Child, while Saint Francis
prayed by Night, faw Chrift and the Virgin
Mary, and many other Saints with Him . 76

Contents.

CHAPTER XVIII.

                                                                         PAGE
Of the marvellous Chapter held by Saint Francis in the Church of St. Mary of the Angels, where were affembled more than five thoufand of the Brethren 78

CHAPTER XIX.

How the Grapes in the Vineyard of the Prieft of Rieti, in whofe Houfe Saint Francis prayed, were trampled and plucked by the many People which came thither to him; and then miraculoufly made more Wine than ever before, even as Saint Francis had promifed. And how the Lord revealed to Saint Francis that Paradife fhould be his lot 85

CHAPTER XX.

Of a very fair Vifion, feen by a young Friar, who held the Cowl in fuch abomination that He was difpofed to lay afide his Habit and forfake the Order 90

CHAPTER XXI.

Of the Moft Holy Miracle, which Saint Francis performed, when he converted the very fierce Wolf at Gubbio 93

CHAPTER XXII.

How Saint Francis tamed the wild Turtle-Doves 99

CHAPTER XXIII.

How Saint Francis set free the Friar who had sinned with the aid of the Devil . . . 101

CHAPTER XXIV.

How Saint Francis converted the Sultan of Babylon to the Faith , ... 103

CHAPTER XXV.

How Saint Francis miraculously healed the Leper in Body and in Soul; and that which the Soul spake, ascending into Heaven . . 106

CHAPTER XXVI.

How Saint Francis converted three Thieves and Murderers, and made them Brethren; and of the most glorious Vision beheld of one of them who was a most holy Brother . 111

CHAPTER XXVII.

How Saint Francis converted two Scholars of Bologna and made Friars of them; and then rid one of them of a sore Temptation which beset him 124

CHAPTER XXVIII.

Of an Ecſtaſy which ſeized upon Brother Bernard and held him from Matins even until Nones, he being all that ſpace unconſcious of Aught 129

CHAPTER XXIX.

How the Devil ofttimes did appear in the Form of One Crucified unto Brother Rufus, telling him that all his Labor was vain, inaſmuch as he was not choſen unto Eternal Life: Saint Francis learning this through Divine Revelation, ſhowed Brother Rufus the Error in which he lay 131

CHAPTER XXX.

Of the glorious Sermon which Saint Francis and Brother Rufus preached at Aſſiſi . . 138

CHAPTER XXXI.

How Saint Francis duly knew the ſecret Souls of all his Brethren 141

CHAPTER XXXII.

How Brother Maximus entreated of Chriſt the Virtue of Meekneſs 143

CHAPTER XXXIII.

How Saint Clara, at the Command of the Pope, bleffed the Bread which was on the Table: whereat on every Loaf was feen the fign of the Holy Crofs 146

CHAPTER XXXIV.

How Saint Louis, King of France, went in Perfon, in the Guife of a Pilgrim, to Perugia, to vifit Holy Brother Guy 148

CHAPTER XXXV.

How, being infirm, Saint Clara was borne by a Miracle unto the Church of Saint Francis, upon Chriftmas Night, and heard Mafs therein 151

CHAPTER XXXVI.

How Saint Francis fet forth to Brother Leo a fair Vifion which he faw 153

CHAPTER XXXVII.

How Jefus Chrift the Bleffed, at the requeft of Saint Francis, did convert a rich and noble Knight, and make him a Monk, the Same having made great Proffers and paid much Honor unto Saint Francis 155

Contents.

CHAPTER XXXVIII.

How Saint Francis had ſpiritual Knowledge that Brother Elias was damned, and was deſtined to die outſide of the Order; wherefore at Brother Elias' Entreaty He prayed to God in his Behalf and was heard . . . 159

CHAPTER XXXIX.

Of the Marvellous Sermon which was preached in the Confiſtory by Saint Antony of Padua, a Gray Friar 163

CHAPTER XL.

Of the Miracle which God performed when Saint Antony, being at Rimini, preached to the Fiſhes of the Sea 165

CHAPTER XLI.

How the Venerable Brother Simon freed from ſore Temptation a Brother which for that ſame cauſe was about to forſake the Order . 169

CHAPTER XLII.

Of the fair Miracles which God wrought through thoſe Holy Brethren, Brother Welcome, Brother Peter of Monticello, and Brother Conrad of Offida: and how Brother

Welcome bore a Leper fifteen Miles in moſt brief Space; and to the one ſpake Saint Michael, and to the other came the Virgin Mary and laid her Son in his Arms 174

CHAPTER XLIII.

How Brother Conrad of Offida did convert a young Monk who afflicted the other Friars. And how the ſaid young Monk, coming to die, did appear to the ſaid Brother Conrad, entreating that he would pray for him: and how he ſet him free by his Prayers from the very great Pains of Purgatory . . 179

CHAPTER XLIV.

How the Mother of Chriſt and Saint John the Evangeliſt did appear unto Brother Conrad, and did tell him which of they twain did grieve moſt ſore for the Paſſion of Chriſt 182

CHAPTER XLV.

Of the Converſion and Life and Miracles and Death of that holy Brother, John of the Pen 185

CHAPTER XLVI.

How Brother Peace, being at Prayer, ſaw the Soul of his Brother, Brother Humility, aſcend to Heaven 193

Contents.

CHAPTER XLVII.

Of that Holy Monk to whom the Mother of Chriſt appeared when he was infirm, and brought him three Boxes of Electuary . . 196

CHAPTER XLVIII.

How Brother James of Maſſa ſaw in a Viſion all the Gray Friars of the World, after the Faſhion of a Tree, and did know the Virtues and the Merits and the Vices of every one 199

CHAPTER XLIX.

How Chriſt appeared to Brother John of Vernia 206

CHAPTER L.

How, ſaying Maſs upon All Souls' Day, Brother John of Vernia ſaw many Souls ſet free from Purgatory 214

CHAPTER LI.

Of the Holy Brother James of Fallerone; and how, before he died, he did appear to Brother John of Vernia 216

CHAPTER LII.

Of the Viſion of Brother John of Vernia, wherein he knew the whole Order of the Holy Trinity 220

CHAPTER LIII.

How, ſaying Maſs, Brother John of Vernia fell as one Dead 222

The Little Flowers
OF
Saint Francis of Assisi.

———◆———

CHAPTER I.

In the Name of Our Lord and Saviour Jesus Christ, Who was crucified, and of His Mother the Virgin Mary. In this Book are contained certain Little Flowers, Miracles, and devout Examples of that glorious poor Follower of Christ, Saint Francis, and of certain of his holy Companions. Told to the Praise of Jesus Christ. Amen.

WE have first to consider that the glorious Saint Francis in all the acts of his life was like unto Christ, our blessed Lord; for even as Christ in the beginning of His preaching chose to Himself twelve Apostles who should renounce all worldly things and follow after Him in poverty and

and in other virtuous deeds, even so Saint Francis chose in the beginning of the foundation of his Order twelve companions, vowed to the most abject poverty; and also even as one of the twelve Apostles of Christ, reproved of God, went out and hanged himself by the neck, so one of the twelve Companions of Saint Francis, the same which was called Brother John of the Chapel, did turn apostate, and finally go out and hang himself by the neck. And this is a worthy example for the elect, and a subject for fear and humility, considering that none can be sure of continuing unto the end in the grace of God. And as those holy Apostles were a wonder to all men for their sanctity and humility, and were filled full with the Holy Ghost, so too the most holy companions of Saint Francis were men of so much sanctity, that, from the days of the Apostles down to the present time, the world has known no such wonderful and holy men, insomuch as a certain one among them was snatched up into the third Heaven, like Saint Paul, and that was Brother Guy; a certain one among them, that is Brother Philip Long, was touched upon the lips by an Angel with a living coal, as was the Prophet

Prophet Ifaiah; a certain one among them, and that was Brother Silvefter, talked with God, as might one friend with another, even as did Mofes; a certain one among them did rife by fubtlety of intellect even unto the light of divine wifdom, like unto the Eagle, which is John the Evangelift, and this was Brother Bernard, the moft humble of men, who did expound the Holy Scriptures moft learnedly; a certain one among them was fanctified of God, and canonized in heaven while ftill living upon this earth, and that was Brother Rufus, a gentleman of Affifi. And thus were all privileged to receive fingular figns of fanctity, even as fhall be fet forth in the following pages.

CHAPTER II.

Of Brother Bernard of Quintavalle, the firft Companion of Saint Francis.

THE firft companion of Saint Francis was one Brother Bernard of Affifi, the fame being converted in this fafhion; Saint Francis being ftill clad in fecular garb, although

though he had already renounced the world, and went about defpifing all vain fhow, and mortifying his flefh by manifold forms of penitence, infomuch that of many he was held to be half mad, and was fcorned as a fool and driven forth with ftones and loathing alike by his family and by ftrangers, and he amidft all infults and injuries remained paffive, as if deaf and dumb, — Bernard of Affifi, who was one of the moft noble, rich, and wife men of that city, began prudently to confider Saint Francis' exceeding contempt for this world and his great patience amid infults; how that for the fpace of two long years, being thus held in abomination and defpifed of all men, he feemed ever but the more fteadfaft in his faith. He began to think and to fay to himfelf, "It can in no wife be but that this Brother is poffeffed of the great grace of God;" and he invited him to fup with him that night and to lodge with him. And Saint Francis accepted his proffers, and fupped and lodged with him. And then did Bernard ponder in his heart and meditate upon his fanctity; whereupon he ordered a bed to be laid for him in his own chamber, wherein a lamp ever burned at night. And Saint Francis defiring

defiring to hide his great fanctity, immediately that he entered the chamber, threw himfelf upon his bed and feigned fleep; and even fo did Bernard, and after a certain fpace he turned himfelf over and began to fnore loudly, as he were fleeping heavily. For the which thing Saint Francis, truly believing that Bernard flept in his firft flumbers, arofe from the bed and fell himfelf upon his knees, lifting both hands and eyes to heaven, and with the utmoft fervor and devotion he exclaimed, "My God! my God!" and thus crying and weeping much, he remained until morning, repeating ever, "My God! my God!" and nought elfe; and thus fpake Saint Francis, contemplating and admiring the excellency of the Divine Majefty Which had deigned to defcend to pardon a perifhing world; wherefore Saint Francis became a poor beggar and devoted his life to feeking out fome means of falvation for his foul and for the fouls of others. And ftill illumined by the Holy Ghoft, or elfe indeed by the fpirit of prophecy, forefeeing the great things which the Lord was to do for him and for his Order, and confidering his own infufficiency and little virtue, he cried aloud and prayed

prayed unto God that of His Charity and Omnipotence, without which human weakneſs availeth nought, He would ſupply, aid, and complete the work which man alone could not achieve.

Bernard, ſeeing by the light of the lamp theſe moſt pious acts of Saint Francis, and conſidering devoutly the words which he uttered, was touched and inſpired of the Holy Ghoſt to change his life; inſomuch that at dawn of day he called unto Saint Francis and ſaid thus: "Brother Francis, my heart is greatly minded to forſake the world and to follow after thee in all things that thou ſhalt command me." Hearing this, Saint Francis rejoiced in ſpirit and ſpake thus: "Bernard, this of which you ſpeak is ſo great and difficult a taſk that we muſt needs take counſel concerning it with Our Lord Jeſus Chriſt, and pray Him that it may pleaſe Him to ſhow us His ſovereign will in the ſame, and to teach us how we may execute it; and therefore let us go forth together to the Epiſcopal Palace, where we may find a righteous prieſt, and we will bid him ſay a maſs; there we will remain and pray even unto the third hour of the day, entreating God that

that even in the three openings of the Miſſal He will ſet forth to us the way which it ſhall pleaſe Him to have us go."

Bernard replied that theſe things liked him well. Thus they ſet forth and came unto the Biſhop's Palace; and there having heard the Maſs, and remained abſorbed in prayer even unto the third hour of the day, the prieſt, at the petition of Saint Francis, took up the Miſſal, and making the ſign of the moſt Holy Croſs, did open it three times in the name of Our Lord Jeſus Chriſt; and at the firſt opening there appeared theſe words, which Chriſt ſpake in the Goſpel unto the young man who aſked of Him the way to be perfect: "If thou wilt be perfect, go and ſell that thou haſt and give to the poor, and come and follow Me." At the ſecond opening there appeared theſe words uttered by Chriſt to the Apoſtles when He ſent them forth to preach: "Provide neither gold, nor ſilver, nor braſs in your purſes, nor ſcrip for your journey, neither two coats, neither ſhoes, nor yet ſtaves;" deſiring thereby to teach them that they ſhould ſet all their truſt in God, and bend their whole thoughts to the preaching of the Holy Goſpel; at the third

third opening of the Miſſal there appeared theſe words which Chriſt ſpake: "If any man will come after Me, let him deny himſelf, and take up his croſs, and follow Me."

Then ſaid Saint Francis to Bernard, "Behold the counſel which Chriſt hath given us. Go therefore and do that which you have heard; and bleſſed be Our Lord Jeſus Chriſt, which hath ſtooped to ſhow us the way of His goſpel." Hearing this, Bernard went out and ſold all that that he had, — and he was very rich, — and with great joy did divide all his wealth among widows and orphans, among priſons and monaſteries, and among hoſpitals and pilgrims; and in all things was aided faithfully and providently of Saint Francis.

And a certain man, whoſe name was Silveſter, ſeeing that Saint Francis gave ſo much money to the poor, and continued to give large ſums, pinched by avarice, ſaid to Saint Francis, "Never yet have you paid me all that you owe me for thoſe ſtones that you did buy to repair the church; now therefore that you have money, pay." Then Saint Francis, marvelling much at his avarice, and loath to contend with him,
like

like unto a true obferver of the Holy Gofpel, did ftretch forth his hand into the lap of Bernard, and drawing it out full of money, caft the fame into the lap of Silvefter, faying, "If more you defire, yet more will I give you." Silvefter being content with that that he had, went away and returned to his own houfe; but at evening, pondering on that which he had done that day, and reproaching himfelf for his avarice, confidering the fervor of Bernard and the fanctity of Saint Francis, the following night, and for yet two other nights, God fent him this rare vifion: that from the mouth of Saint Francis there iffued forth a crofs of gold, the top of which reached even unto Heaven, and the arms of which ftretched from the Eaft even unto the Weft. Becaufe of this vifion he gave away for love of God all that that he had, and became one of the Gray Friars; and fuch were his fanctity and grace while in the Order, that he fpake with God even as one friend with another, as Saint Francis many times experienced, and as is by him fet forth in thefe pages.

Bernard likewife received great grace from God, forafmuch as he was often tranfported

ported in the contemplation of God; and Saint Francis said of him that he was worthy of all reverence, and that he was the true founder of this Order, inasmuch as he was the first who forsook the world, keeping nothing for himself, but giving all to Christ's poor; and he set an example of Christian poverty, offering himself naked to the arms of Christ crucified; for which thing may he be blessed *in saecula saeculorum.* Amen.

CHAPTER III.

How for the evil Thoughts which Saint Francis had regarding Brother Bernard, he commanded that same Brother Bernard that three Times he should place his Feet upon his Neck and upon his Mouth.

THAT most devout servant of the Cross, Saint Francis, from severe penance and constant tears had become almost blind and saw but little. Upon one occasion he left the place where he abode and went to that place where Brother Bernard sojourned, to speak with him of divine things. And coming to that place he learned that the

the Brother was at prayer in the wood, rapt, and conjoined with God. Then Saint Francis went forth into that wood and called aloud, ſaying, " Come hither and ſpeak to this blind beggar." And Brother Bernard anſwered him not, foraſmuch as, being a man greatly given to meditation, his mind was abſorbed in the contemplation of God; and he was ſtrangely favored in converſe with God, as Saint Francis had ofttimes proven, and therefore did he deſire to have ſpeech with him. After a certain ſpace he called unto him a ſecond and even a third time after the ſame faſhion; and never once did Brother Bernard heed or hear his voice; neither did he make any anſwer, nor came he forth to meet him; ſo that Saint Francis departed no little diſconſolate, and marvelling and lamenting in his own mind that Brother Bernard, three times called, came not forth to him. Journeying thence with theſe thoughts, Saint Francis, having gone but a little way, ſaid unto his companion, "Await me here." And he went aſide into a ſolitary place and fell to praying, beſeeching God that He would reveal to him wherefore Brother Bernard made not anſwer unto him. And

ſtanding

standing there, he heard a voice from God which spake these words: "O poor weak soul, why art thou disturbed? Should man leave God for his fellow man? Brother Bernard, when you cried unto him, was conjoined with Me, and hence he could not come to thee, neither could he make answer unto thee; therefore marvel not that he answered thee not, since his soul was so far removed from his body that he heard not any of thy words." Saint Francis, having this answer from God, immediately returned again with much speed to Brother Bernard, humbly to accuse himself of the evil thoughts which he had cherished towards him. And seeing him draw nigh, Brother Bernard went out to meet him and fell down before him; and then Saint Francis raised him up, and with all humility told his thoughts, and the trouble which he had felt concerning him, and how that God had made answer unto him in the matter; hence he concluded thus: "I charge you by your sacred vow of obedience that you do do the things which I shall command you." Brother Bernard, fearing lest Saint Francis should require of him some excessive thing, as was his wont, made honest endeavor

endeavor to avoid this obedience, anſwering thus: "I am prepared to obey you meekly, if you will promiſe me to do that which I in turn ſhall command of you." And Saint Francis promiſing him, Brother Bernard ſaid, "Speak, father; bid me what you would have me to do." Then ſaid Saint Francis: "I command you, by your ſacred vow of obedience, that, to puniſh my preſumption and the boldneſs of my heart, now as I throw myſelf flat upon the ground you place one foot upon my neck and the other upon my mouth, and thus ſhall you paſs three times over my body, crying ſhame upon me and reviling me; and more eſpecially ſhall you cry unto me, 'Lie there, thou vile ſon of Peter Bernardone; whence haſt thou acquired ſuch pride, vileſt of all creatures that thou art?'" Hearing this, Brother Bernard, hard as was his taſk, yet for the ſake of his ſacred vow of obedience, as courteouſly as he might, did fulfil the will of Saint Francis, even as he had commanded him; and this done, Saint Francis ſaid: "Do you command me now in turn whatſoever you will that I ſhall do, inaſmuch as I have promiſed obedience." Then ſaid Brother Bernard, "By your ſacred vow of of obedience I charge you that as many times as we may hap to be in company you do reprove me and correct me sharply for my sins." At which thing Saint Francis marvelled greatly, seeing that Brother Bernard was a man of great sanctity whom he held in much reverence, nor did he hold him censurable for any sin whatsoever. And although from that time forth Saint Francis strove to spend much time with him in accordance with his vow of obedience, never any word of reproof or blame passed his lips toward one whom he knew to be a man of such great sanctity; but as often as he desired to see him, or indeed to hear him converse with God, as speedily as might be he went forth unto him; and it was most devout to see with how great love and reverence and humility Father Saint Francis used to speak with Brother Bernard his first-born son. To the praise and glory of Jesus Christ, and of that poor Christian, Francis. Amen.

CHAPTER IV.

How the Angel of the Lord put a Queſtion unto Brother Elias, the Keeper of a certain Convent in the Vale of Spoleto, and foraſmuch as Brother Elias made Anſwer haughtily, departed thence and went forth unto St. James of Compoſtella, where he met with Brother Bernard and told his Tale unto him.

AT the beginning and firſt undertaking of the Order, when the Friars were but few, and but little land had been acquired, Saint Francis, from a ſpirit of devotion, did go to St. James of Galicia, and in his train were certain Brethren, of whom one was Brother Bernard. And travelling thus their road, they met a poor ſick beggar, having pity upon whom, Saint Francis ſaid to Brother Bernard: "Son, I beſeech you, ſtay here and ſerve this ſick man." And Brother Bernard, humbly kneeling and bowing his head, yielded obedience to the Holy Father and remained in that ſpot; and Saint Francis with his companions went his way unto St. James. Coming thither and ſpending the night in prayer within

within the Church of St. James, it was revealed of God to Saint Francis that he was deſtined to acquire much land throughout the world, inaſmuch as his Order was deſtined to ſpread and to grow even unto a vaſt multitude of Monks; and in accordance with this revelation Saint Francis forthwith began to acquire land in that ſame region. And travelling homeward by that ſelfſame way he came, Saint Francis met with Brother Bernard and the ſick man with whom he left him, healed and made quite whole; hence Saint Francis granted Brother Bernard in the enſuing year that he alſo ſhould viſit St. James.

And thus Saint Francis returned into the Vale of Spoleto. And here he ſojourned in a deſolate place, he and Brother Maximus and Brother Elias and others. And every man among them ſtrove mightily leſt he ſhould peſter or annoy Saint Francis as he prayed; and this they did for the great reverence which they bare him, and foraſmuch as they were well aware that God made known unto him great wonders in his prayers. It befell one day that Saint Francis being at prayer in the wood, a Beauteous Youth arrayed for a journey came to to the door of that place wherein he ſtayed, and knocked ſo often and ſo loud and for ſo long a ſpace, that much the brothers marvelled among themſelves at ſuch unwonted noiſe. Brother Maximus went out and oped the door and ſaid to that youth, "Whence come you, O Son, ſince it ſeems you never did come hither yet, inaſmuch as you knock thus contrary to all uſe?" The youth made anſwer: "And how ſhould I knock?" Then ſaid Brother Maximus, "Knock thrice, the one knock following ſlowly after the other; then wait ſo long as until the Brother ſhall have ſaid a Paternoster and come unto you; and if after that ſpace he come not, knock yet once again." The young man anſwered, "My haſte is exceeding great, foraſmuch as I have a long journey to make, and am come hither to ſpeak with Brother Francis; but he now is in the wood loft in a muſe, and hence I will not vex him; but go call me hither Brother Elias, to whom I would put but one queſtion only, ſince I hear that he is very wiſe." Brother Maximus went in and bade Brother Elias go out to the young man; and he waxed angry and would not go. At which thing Brother Maximus

Maximus knew not what to do, neither what anfwer he fhould make to him, inafmuch as faying that Brother Elias could not come, he fpake falfely; faying he was vexed in fpirit and would not come, he feared left he fhould fet an evil example. And Brother Maximus lingering thus, the young man knocked yet again as before, and in a little time Brother Maximus returned to the gate, and faid to the young man, "Why heed you not my counfels in your knocking?" The young man anfwered: "Brother Elias comes not unto me; go therefore and fay to Brother Francis that I am come hither to fpeak with him; but forafmuch as I would not come againft him in his praying, let him bid Brother Elias come out to me." And then Brother Maximus went in to Saint Francis, who was praying in the thick wood with his face lift up to heaven, and he delivered the young man's meffage and the anfwer of Brother Elias; and that young man was the Angel of the Lord in the likenefs of a Man. Then Saint Francis, removing not from his place, neither cafting down his eyes, faid to Brother Maximus: "Go, fay unto Brother Elias, by his vow of obedience

I charge him that he ſhall go forthwith to that young man." Brother Elias, hearing Saint Francis' charge of obedience, went out to the gate greatly troubled, and with fury and noiſe did open it, and ſpake to the young man, ſaying, "What would you with me?" The young man made anſwer, ſaying, "Beware, Brother, leſt you be troubled in ſpirit even as you ſeem; for anger clouds the mind, letting it not ſee the Truth." Then ſaid Brother Elias, "Tell me what you would with me." The young man made anſwer, "I aſk you whether it be lawful for followers of the Holy Scriptures to eat that which is ſet before them, even as Chriſt ſpake to his diſciples; and I aſk you alſo whether it be lawful for any man to ſet before them aught that is contrary to Chriſtian freedom?" Brother Elias made anſwer loftily: "Well might I anſwer your queſtion, but I will not do ſo; go your way." The young man ſaid, "Better can I anſwer this queſtion than can you." Then Brother Elias, vexed and angered, cloſed the gate and went thence. Going in, he began to ponder upon the ſaid queſtions, and to doubt within himſelf concerning them, and he knew not how to ſolve them

them, notwithstanding that he was Vicar-General of the Order, and had commanded and writ in the Rule, contrary to the gospel and contrary to the Rule of Saint Francis, that no brother of the Order should eat meat; so that the said question was expressly directed against him. Thus, knowing not how to dissipate his doubts, and considering the modesty of the Youth, and how that he had said He could better answer the question than he, he turned back to the gate and opened it to ask of the Youth the aforesaid question; but he had already journeyed thence, forasmuch as the proud spirit of Brother Elias was not worthy to hold converse with the Angel.

This done, Saint Francis, to whom all things were revealed of God, returned from the wood, and with a loud voice reviled Brother Elias, saying, "Ill have you done, O proud Brother Elias, for you have driven hence from our midst holy Angels who came hither to counsel and instruct. I tell you that I fear exceeding much lest your pride lead you not forth at last from this Order." And even so it fell out, as Saint Francis had said, inasmuch as he died outside the Order.

In

In that fame day and in the felfsame hour when that Angel departed thence, He appeared in the felfsame form unto Brother Bernard, who was travelling back from St. James, and ftood on the fhores of a vaft ftream, and greeted him in his own tongue, faying, "God grant you His peace, O good Brother." And good Brother Bernard, marvelling much, and confidering the fair face of the Youth and the fpeech of his own land with that peaceful greeting and joyous countenance, he afked him: "Whence come you, good Youth?" The Angel anfwering faid, "I come from that fame place where dwells Saint Francis, and I travelled thither to have fpeech of him; but I could not, he being in the thick woods loft in contemplation of things divine, and I was loath to vex him. And in that fame place dwell alfo Brother Maximus and Brother Guy and Brother Elias; and Brother Maximus bade me knock at the gate like unto a Friar; but Brother Elias, although at firft he would not anfwer me concerning the queftion which I put to him, yet after did repent him fore and would fain have heard me and feen me and he could not." After thefe words the Angel fpake to Brother

Brother Bernard, faying, "Why crofs you not over yonder ftream?" Brother Bernard made anfwer: "Forafmuch as I fear the dangers of the deep waters which I fee." The Angel faid, "We will pafs over together, nothing doubting." And He took his hand, and in the twinkling of an eye He put him on the farther fide of the ftream. Then Brother Bernard knew that this was the Angel of the Lord, and with great awe and gladnefs he cried aloud, "O bleffed Angel of the Lord, declare unto me your name." The Angel anfwered and faid, "Why afk you me my name, which is Wonderful?" And faying this the Angel vanifhed, leaving Brother Bernard much comforted, infomuch fo that he travelled all his road with great rejoicing; and he was mindful of the day and the hour in which the Angel had appeared unto him. And coming unto that place where Saint Francis abode with his chofen Companions, he told them all in due order; and he knew for a certainty that that fame Angel in the felfsame day and hour had appeared to him and them.

CHAPTER V.

How that Saint, Brother Bernard of Aſſiſi, was deſpatched by Saint Francis to Bologna, and there took up his Abode.

INASMUCH as Saint Francis and his companions were called of God and choſen to bear in their hearts and in their lives, and to preach with their tongues, the Croſs of Chriſt, they both ſeemed and were men who crucified the fleſh, alike in their habit and in their auſtere life, alike in their every act and deed; and nevertheleſs they deſired the rather to endure ſhame and opprobrium for the love of Chriſt than to receive worldly honors, or reverence, or the praiſe of men: thus injuries rejoiced them and honors afflicted them; and thus they paſſed through the world as Pilgrims and Strangers, bearing with them nought ſave Chriſt Crucified; and yet they were the true Vine, which is Chriſt, bringing forth great and good ſpiritual fruit, which they garnered in for God. It happened in the firſt days of the Order that Saint Francis ſent Brother Bernard forth to Bologna, to the

the end that there he might bear fruit unto God, according to the grace given him of Our Lord; and Brother Bernard, making the sign of the moſt Holy Croſs, and mindful of his ſacred vow of obedience, departed thence and came unto Bologna; and the children, ſeeing him in worn and tattered raiment, mocked at him and reviled him as they might have any clown; and Brother Bernard patiently and cheerfully bore all things for the love of Jeſus Chriſt; nay, rather that the more he might be chaſtened, ſtudiouſly did ſeat himſelf in the market-place, where ſitting, there ſoon flocked round about him many boys and men, who pulled him by the cowl, ſome before and ſome behind, ſome caſt duſt upon him and ſome ſtones, ſome thruſt and ſhoved him here and ſome there; and Brother Bernard bore all things with patience and meekneſs, and with a ſmiling face, murmuring not, neither complaining; and, moreover, often he returned to that ſame place ſolely to ſuffer ſimilar things for the good of his Soul. And albeit Patience have her perfect work and be a token of Virtue, a learned doctor of laws, ſeeing and conſidering ſo much conſtancy and valor in Brother Bernard, ſuffering for ſo many days unmoved by by any blows or pinches, ſaid to himſelf, "Verily, it cannot be but that is a holy man;" and drawing near to him, he queſtioned him thus: "Who art thou, and wherefore haſt thou come hither?" And Brother Bernard for all anſwer put his hand into his boſom and drew forth the Rule of Saint Francis, and gave it to him that he might read; and having read, conſidering his extreme ſtate of Perfection, with the utmoſt wonder and admiration he turned to his companions and ſaid, "Verily, this is the moſt high ſtate of religion of which I have heard; and this man and his companions are the moſt holy men in all the earth, and he who harms the leaſt among them is guilty of a very grievous ſin; for every man among them ſhould be held in high honor, inaſmuch as he is the true friend of God." And he ſpake to Brother Bernard, ſaying, "If you will abide among us, where you may ſerve God acceptably, I for the ſalvation of my ſoul will joyfully give you an abiding-place." Brother Bernard made anſwer: "Sir, methinks your words are inſpired of Our Lord Jeſus Chriſt; and I cheerfully accept this your offer, to the honor and glory of Chriſt." Then the ſaid

said Judge with great joy and lovingkindness led Brother Bernard to his house, and there bestowed upon him the promised lodging, and set it in order, and provided for all his costs; and shortly after he himself became a Father, and the especial ally and champion of Brother Bernard and of his companions. And Brother Bernard, for this his holy conversion, began to be much honored of all men, insomuch that they who might touch the hem of his garments, or could but look upon him, held themselves blest; but he, as a true disciple of Christ, and of the meek and lowly Francis, fearing lest worldly honors should mar the peace and safety of his soul, departed thence one day and returned to Saint Francis and spake these words: "Father, an abiding-place is found in the city of Bologna: I prithee send thither Brothers who may maintain it, and let them sojourn there, forasmuch as I no longer profit you aught in that spot; indeed, for the exceeding honor which is paid me I fear lest I lose more than I gain." Then Saint Francis, hearing all things in due order, how Our Lord had wrought a great work through Brother Bernard, praised and thanked God, Who

Who thus deigned to increaſe the number of poor followers of the Croſs: and then he ſent forth his Companions into Bologna and into Lombardy, who acquired much land in many places.

CHAPTER VI.

How Saint Francis bleſſed Brother Bernard, and made him his Vicar when he came to paſs away from this Life.

SO great was the ſanctity of Brother Bernard, that Saint Francis reverenced him much, and many times did praiſe him. Saint Francis once being devoutly rapt in prayer, it was revealed to him of God that Brother Bernard was by Divine Leave to ſuſtain many and valiant battles with the demons; hence Saint Francis, having exceeding great compaſſion upon the ſaid Brother Bernard, whom he loved as he were his own ſon, he prayed many days with tears, entreating God for him, and recommending him to Chriſt Jeſus, that he might give him victory over the demon. And Saint Francis, praying thus devoutly, God one day made anſwer unto him: "Francis, fear not;

not; forafmuch as all the temptations by which Brother Bernard is to be affailed are allowed of God as a teft of his valor and a Crown of Glory, and finally he fhall triumph over all his enemies, forafmuch as he is one of the Commiffaries of the kingdom of Heaven." At the which anfwer Saint Francis rejoiced greatly, and praifed the Lord; and from that time forth his love and reverence waxed ever greater. And well he proved them, not only in his life, but alfo in his death. Forafmuch as Saint Francis, being about to die, even as that holy Patriarch Jacob, his mourning fons ftanding about him devoutly, weeping at the departure of fo amiable a father, he afked them, "Where is my Firftborn? Come hither to me, my Son, that my Soul may blefs thee before I die." Then Brother Bernard faid privily to Brother Elias, who was the Vicar of the Order, "Father, go thou to the right hand of the Saint, that he may blefs thee." And Brother Elias, placing himfelf upon his right hand, Saint Francis, who had loft his fight by reafon of his many tears, laid his right hand upon the head of Brother Elias and faid, "This is not the head of my firftborn fon, Brother Bernard

Bernard." Then Brother Bernard went and ſtood by his left hand; and Saint Francis ſtretching forth his arms in the form of a Croſs, laid his right hand upon the head of Brother Bernard and his left hand upon the head of that ſame Brother Elias, and ſaid to Brother Bernard: "May God the Father and Our Lord Jeſus Chriſt bleſs thee with every ſpiritual bleſſing, and may Chriſt grant thee all celeſtial bleſſings, even as thou art the Firſtborn, choſen into this Holy Order to give a godly example, to follow Chriſt in Chriſtian poverty; inaſmuch as thou haſt given not only all that which was thine, dividing it wholly and freely among the poor for the love of Chriſt, but alſo haſt given thyſelf a free-will offering unto God in this Order, a ſacrifice pleaſing in His ſight. Receive, therefore, the bleſſing of Our Lord Jeſus Chriſt, and of me, His poor ſervant, bleſſings everlaſting, whether walking, ſtanding, waking, ſleeping, living, or dying; and all who ſhall bleſs thee ſhall themſelves be filled with bleſſing. They who curſe thee ſhall not go unpuniſhed. Thou art chief among all thy Brethren, and all the Brothers ſhall bow to thy will. Thou haſt my leave to receive
into

into the Order whomſoever thou wilt; and no Brother ſhall have ſupremacy over thee, and thou art free to come and go whitherſoever thou wilt." And after the death of Saint Francis the Brethren loved and revered Brother Bernard as a venerable Father; and he, coming to die, many Brothers gathered about him from all quarters of the globe, among them being that divine hierarch Brother Guy, who, seeing Brother Bernard, cried aloud, with great gladneſs, "*Lift up your heart, Brother Bernard; lift up your heart.*" And Brother Bernard bade one of the Brethren privily that he ſhould prepare a place meet for contemplation for Brother Guy; and ſo it was done. Brother Bernard, being at the laſt hour of his death, bade his Brethren lift him up, and ſpake to ſuch of them as were there preſent, ſaying: "My beloved Brethren, I have not many words to ſpeak to you. But you muſt be mindful that that degree of Religion which I have had you have at this preſent, and unto that which I now enjoy, you ſhall yet attain; and I tell you from my ſoul of ſouls that I would not for a thouſand Worlds like unto this have ſerved other Lord than Our Lord Jeſus Chriſt.

Chrift. And for every offence that I have committed I confefs myfelf guilty, and accufe myfelf before my Saviour Jefus and before you. I befeech you, my deareft Brethren, love one another." And after thefe words, and other wholefome teachings, he laid himfelf down upon his bed, his face fhone with joy and fplendor fo exceeding that all the Brothers marvelled greatly, and in that rapture his moft faintly foul, crowned with glory, paffed from this prefent life into the bleffed life of the angels.

CHAPTER VII.

How Saint Francis fafted forty Days and forty Nights in an Ifland of the Lake of Perugia, eating no more but half a Loaf.

THAT true fervant of Chrift, Saint Francis, being in certain things almoft another Chrift, fent into the world to fave the nations, Our Lord and Father God defired to make him in many acts conformable and like unto His Son Jefus Chrift; even as we have feen in the venerable College of the twelve Companions,

panions, and in the admirable Myſtery of the Sacred Stigmata, and in the Faſt laſting throughout the whole term of Lent, which took place after this manner: Saint Francis being once, upon the laſt day of the Carnival, beſide the Lake of Perugia in the houſe of one of his devout followers, with whom he had tarried for a night, he was inſpired of God that he ſhould proceed to keep his faſt in an Iſland of that lake; wherefore Saint Francis prayed this his follower that for the love of Chriſt he would bear him over in his boat unto an Iſland of the lake where no man abode; this he ſhould do upon the night of Aſh Wedneſday, in ſuch manner that they might be ſeen of none; and he for love of the great devotion which he felt for Saint Francis faithfully did his beheſt, and bare him over to the Iſland: and Saint Francis took nothing with him ſave two ſmall loaves. And having come to the Iſland, and his friend departing thence to return to his houſe, Saint Francis charged him by the love which he bare him that he ſhould reveal to no man where he did lie, and that he ſhould not journey back to fetch him ſooner than Maundy-Thurſday;
and

and thus they parted. And Saint Francis abode there alone; and there being no habitation wherein he might find ſhelter, he entered into a thick wood wherein many thorns and brambles and little buſhes had formed a den or burrow, and herein he fell to praying and to muſing upon celeſtial things. And herein he ſtayed during the whole ſpace of Lent, eating not, neither drinking aught, ſave the half of one of thoſe ſmall loaves, according as his faithful follower found him when he croſſed over to him on Maundy-Thurſday; the which found of two ſmall loaves one entire, and of the other half; it is believed that Saint Francis did partake out of reverence for the faſting of the bleſſed Chriſt, Who faſted forty days and forty nights, partaking of no bodily food; and thus with that half loaf he drove far from him the venom of Vainglory, and following after Chriſt faſted forty days and forty nights. And then in that place where Francis did ſuch marvellous feats of abſtinence God the Lord wrought many miracles through his merits: for the which thing men began to build houſes there and to dwell there; and in a brief ſpace a Caſtle good and great ſtood

ſtood therein, and this was the home of the Brethren, and it was called by the name of the Iſland; and even unto this preſent time the men and the women of that Caſtle diſplay great reverence and devotion upon that ſpot where Saint Francis faſted as has been here ſet forth.

CHAPTER VIII.

How Saint Francis and Brother Leo, as they journeyed, diſcourſed of Perfect Bliſs.

SAINT FRANCIS once journeying from Perugia to St. Mary of the Angels with Brother Leo in winter time, and the very great cold pinching him ſore, he called aloud to Brother Leo, who walked before, and ſaid thus: "Brother Leo, although the Gray Friars in every place ſet a good example of ſanctity and of godly leſſons, nevertheleſs I deſire you to write down and diligently to note that they know not perfect bliſs." And Saint Francis journeying yet farther, a ſecond time he called aloud, "O Brother Leo, albeit the Gray Friar be eyes to the blind, deliver men from evil, drive out demons, be ears to the deaf, and
feet

feet to the lame, a tongue to the dumb, and what is yet more do reſtore the dead to life within the ſpace of four days, yet write that he knows not perfect bliſs." And journeying yet a little farther, he cried with a loud voice, "O Brother Leo, if the Gray Friar know all tongues, all knowledge, and all the Scriptures in ſuch faſhion that he may propheſy and reveal not alone the things of the future, but even alſo the ſecrets of all conſciences and of all ſouls, ſtill I bid thee write, herein lies not perfect bliſs." Going yet a little farther, Saint Francis called aloud yet once again: "O Brother Leo, Lamb of God, even though the Gray Friar ſpeak with the tongues of men and of angels, and know the courſe of the ſtars and the virtues of all herbs, and were all the treaſures of the earth laid bare to him, and did he know the virtues of birds and fiſhes, and of all animals and of men and of trees and of ſtones and of roots and of waters, ſtill write that herein lies not perfect bliſs." And journeying yet a little ſpace Saint Francis cried aloud: "O Brother Leo, even could the Gray Friar preach ſo well as that he ſhould turn all infidels to the faith of Chriſt, yet write, herein

herein lies not perfect blifs." And this difcourfe enduring for full two miles, Brother Leo with amazement afked him, faying, "Father, I pray thee, for God's fake, that thou wilt tell me where may perfect blifs be found?" And Saint Francis made anfwer thus: "When we fhall have come unto St. Mary of the Angels, dripping with rain and frozen with cold and befpattered with mud and tormented fore with hunger, and fhall knock at the door of that place, and the porter fhall look forth in wrath, and fhall fay, 'Who are ye?' and we fhall fay, 'We be two of your Brethren;' and he fhall fay, 'You fpeak not truly; forfooth you are two ribald knaves who go about deceiving folk and ftealing alms from the poor, get you gone!' and he fhall not open unto us, and fhall leave us ftanding without in the fnow and the wet with cold and hunger even till the fall of night; then if we fhall patiently endure fuch great injuftice and cruelty and villanous rebuffs without peevifhnefs or turbulence, murmuring not againft him, and fhall think humbly and charitably that verily that doorkeeper reads us aright, that our Lord hath bade him revile us and
fpeak

speak againſt us, then, O Brother Leo, mayſt thou write, herein lies perfect bliſs. And if we ſhall perſevere our knocking, and he ſhall come forth in his wrath and drive us thence as raſcals, with ſtripes and revilings, ſaying, 'Get you hence, vileſt thieves, get you to the hoſpital, for here you ſhall not abide, neither ſhall you eat,— if we ſhall endure the ſame meekly and with rejoicing and love, O Brother Leo, then mayſt thou write that herein lies perfect bliſs. And if we, urged by hunger and cold and by the darkneſs, ſhall ſtill perſiſt our knocking and ſhall cry aloud and entreat him for the love of God with much weeping and wailing that he will open and let us in, and he, ſcandalized yet more, ſhall ſay, 'Theſe are importunate knaves, I will chaſtiſe them as is meet; and ſhall come forth with a knotty ſtaff, and ſhall ſeize us by the hair of the head and caſt us to the ground, and roll us in the ſnow, and beat us knot by knot with that ſame ſtaff,— if all theſe things patiently and cheerfully we do endure, thinking upon the ſufferings of the bleſſed Chriſt, which greatly are we bounden to ſuffer for His ſake, O Brother Leo, then mayſt thou write that herein and
in

in this lies perfect blifs. And yet hearken unto the end, Brother Leo. Beyond all the graces and gifts of the Holy Ghoft, which Chrift has granted unto His faithful friends, is victory over felf, and power for love of Chrift to fuffer pain and infult, poverty and difgrace; forafmuch as in all the other gifts of God we can take no pride, they being not our own but of God. Hence the Apoftle faith, 'What have ye which is not of God? And if it be of Him, wherefore do ye glory in it, as if ye had it of your own felves?' But in the crofs of forrow and grief we may glory, inafmuch as the Apoftle faith, 'God forbid that I fhould glory, fave in the crofs of Chrift.'"

CHAPTER IX.

How Saint Francis taught Brother Leo to make Anfwer unto Him: and He could never Speak fave the Contrary of that which Saint Francis Willed.

SAINT FRANCIS being once, in the firft days of the Order, with Brother Leo in a place where they had no books to fay the divine offices, when the hour for Matins was

was at hand, Saint Francis ſaid to Brother Leo: "My beloved, we have no breviary from which to ſay Matins, but in order that we may ſpend the time duly in praiſing God, I will recite and do you reſpond as I ſhall teach you; and beware leſt you change the words diverſely from that which I ſhall teach you. I will ſay thus: 'O Brother Francis, ſo much evil haſt thou done, and ſo many ſins haſt thou committed in this world, that thou art worthy of Hell-fire.' And you, Brother Leo, muſt reſpond: 'Verily, verily thou art deſerving of the hotteſt fires of Hell.'" And Brother Leo, with the ſimplicity of the dove, replied, "I am ready, Father; begin, in the name of God." Then Saint Francis began to ſay, "O Brother Francis, ſo much evil haſt thou done, and ſo many ſins haſt thou committed in this world, that thou art worthy of Hell-fire." And Brother Leo replied, "The Lord ſhall work for thee ſuch miracles that thou ſhalt go ſtraight to Paradiſe." Then ſaid Saint Francis, "Say not ſo, Brother Leo; but when I ſay, 'Brother Francis, thou haſt ſinned grievouſly againſt God, and art worthy to be curſed of God,' you muſt make anſwer thus: 'Verily

'Verily, verily thou art worthy of a place among the Accurſed.'" And Brother Leo replied, "I am ready, Father." Then Saint Francis, with many tears and groans and much beating of his breaſt, cried aloud, "O Lord my God, Lord of heaven and of earth, I have committed ſuch ſins againſt Thee, and ſuch iniquities, that I am worthy to be curſed of Thee." And Brother Leo made anſwer, "O Brother Francis, God ſhall do ſuch things for thee that thou ſhalt be ſingularly bleſſed among the bleſſed." And Saint Francis marvelling that Brother Leo anſwered ever the contrary of that which he had charged him, eſſayed once more, ſaying, "Why anſwer you not as I bid you? I charge you by your holy vow of obedience that you make anſwer as I ſhall direct you. I will ſay thus: 'O wretched Brother Francis, doſt thou think that God will have mercy upon thee, who haſt committed ſuch great ſins againſt the Father of all Mercies and the God of Conſolation that thou art no more worthy to find favor in His ſight?' And you, Brother Leo, ſheep of my flock, muſt make anſwer, 'In no manner art thou worthy to find favor in His ſight.'" But ſo ſoon as Saint Francis ſaid, faid, "O wretched Brother Francis," etc., Brother Leo replied: "Our Heavenly Father, whofe mercy is infinitely greater than are thy fins, will have mercy upon thee and will pour His grace upon thee." At this anfwer Saint Francis was gently enraged and meekly difturbed, faying to Brother Leo, "And wherefore do you make fo bold to act contrary to your vow of obedience, and have fo many times made anfwer contrary to that which I charged you to fay?" Brother Leo replied very humbly and reverently, "God the Lord knoweth the why and the wherefore, my Father, for every time I have fchooled my heart to anfwer as you did bid me; but the Lord made me fpeak as beft it pleafed Him, and not according as was pleafing in my fight." At which thing Saint Francis marvelled, and faid to Brother Leo, "I pray you moft lovingly that this time you anfwer me as I do bid you." Brother Leo replied, "Say on, in God's name, for affuredly I will now make anfwer as you would have me." And Saint Francis, weeping, faid, "O wicked Brother Francis, doft thou think that God will fhow mercy unto thee?" Brother Leo anfwered him, faying, "Ay, and great grace fhalt ſhalt thou have of God. He ſhall exalt thee, and glorify thee in all ages, foraſmuch as he who humbleth himſelf ſhall be exalted; and I can ſpeak no otherwiſe than I do, foraſmuch as God Himſelf ſpeaks through my mouth." And thus in this humble ſtrife, with many tears and with much ſpiritual conſolation, they watched until day.

CHAPTER X.

How Brother Maximus Mockingly ſaid unto Saint Francis that the World was at his Feet. And he made anſwer that this was by the Grace of God, and a Diſgrace to the World.

SAINT FRANCIS ſojourning upon a time in the Convent of Portiuncula with Brother Maximus of Marignano, a man of much ſanctity, diſcretion, and grace in diſcourſing of God, for the which thing greatly did Saint Francis love him, one day Saint Francis returning from the thick wood and from prayer, and being upon the outſkirts of that woody wild, that ſame Brother Maximus, deſiring to know whether his humility were unfeigned, went forth to meet him by the

the way, and mockingly cried out to him, "Wherefore after thee? Wherefore after thee? Wherefore after thee?" Saint Francis aſked, "What ſay you?" Then ſaid Brother Maximus, "I ſay, wherefore followeth the whole world after thee, and why doth every man deſire to ſee and to hear and to obey thee? Thou art not fair to ſee, thou haſt no great learning, neither art thou noble; wherefore, then, doth the whole world follow after thee?" Hearing this, Saint Francis, greatly rejoiced in ſpirit, lifting his face to Heaven, ſtood for a ſpace with his mind fixed on God, and then coming back to earth he knelt and gave praiſe and glory to God, and then with very fervent ſpirit he turned to Brother Maximus and ſaid, "Would you know wherefore men follow after me? Would you know wherefore men follow after me? Would you know wherefore men follow after me? This grace I have from the eyes of the Moſt High God, which in all places behold the godly and the ungodly: foraſmuch as thoſe moſt holy eyes never yet beheld of ſinners one more vile, nor more inſufficient, nor a greater ſinner than am I; nor yet to do that marvellous work which

which He willeth to accomplifh has He found a viler creature upon earth. And therefore hath He chofen me, to confound the Nobility and the Grandeur and the Strength and the Beauty and the Wifdom of the world, to the end that it may be made known that all Virtue and all Goodnefs are from Him and not from His creatures, and that none may glory in his own fight; but that all who glory may glory in the Lord, unto whom be all glory and honor for ever and ever. Amen." Then Brother Maximus at fo humble an anfwer, uttered with fuch fervor, was affrighted, and knew of a furety that the humility of Saint Francis was unfeigned.

CHAPTER XI.

How Saint Francis caufed Brother Maximus to turn Himfelf about, and then departed unto Sienna.

SAINT FRANCIS one day journeying with Brother Maximus, that fame Brother Maximus walking a few paces before, and coming unto a fpot where three roads met, the

the which led to Florence, to Sienna, and to Arezzo, Brother Maximus ſpake thus: "Father, which road ſhall we purſue?" Saint Francis made anſwer, "By that which God chooſeth." Then ſaid Brother Maximus, "And how may we know the will of God?" Saint Francis replied, "By that ſelfſame ſign which I ſhall ſhow you; wherefore I charge you by the fruits of holy obedience that at this meeting-place of the roads, in the very ſpot whereon your feet now reſt, you do turn yourſelf about, even as do children, and give not over turning until I do bid thee ceaſe." Forthwith Brother Maximus began to turn and to twirl himſelf round about; and ſo long did he turn, that at laſt from ſheer dizzineſs, ſuch as ſuch twirling is wont to generate, he fell often to the ground: but Saint Francis not bidding him to ceaſe, and he deſiring faithfully to obey, roſe ever and again to his feet. Finally, as he turned valiantly, Saint Francis cried out, "Stand ſtill, and move not." And he ſtood ſtill, and Saint Francis queſtioned him, ſaying, "Towards what land do you look?" Brother Maximus anſwered, "Towards Sienna." Saint Francis ſaid, "That way God

God wills us to go." Travelling that way, Brother Maximus marvelled that Saint Francis had made him do ſuch things, even as do children at play, in the ſight of thoſe laymen who paſſed along that road. Nevertheleſs, ſo great was his reverence that he ventured not to ſpeak to the Holy Father. Coming near to Sienna, the people of that city heard of the coming of the Saint, and went forth to meet him; and from devotion they bore him and his Companion even unto the Epiſcopal Palace in their arms, ſo that they touched not earth with their feet. In that ſame hour certain men of Sienna ſtrove together, and two of them already lay dead. Saint Francis being in their midſt, preached unto them ſo devoutly and ſo holily that he reſtored them all, every man among them, to peace and great unity and mutual concord; for the which thing the Biſhop of Sienna, hearing of this holy work which Saint Francis had wrought, invited him to his own houſe, and received him with extremeſt honor that day and even for the night. And the next morning Saint Francis, being truly humble, ſeeking never any glory for his works, ſave only the glory of God, roſe betimes with his

his Companion and departed unknown to the Bifhop. At which the faid Brother Maximus murmured within himfelf as he journeyed, faying as he went, "What things are thefe which this good man does? He makes me turn and twirl like any filly child; and to the Bifhop, who has done him fuch honor, he fpeaks no word, neither thanks him, and it feemeth to Brother Maximus as if Saint Francis thus had borne himfelf indifcreetly." But then by divine infpiration returning unto himfelf, and chiding himfelf in the filence of his own heart, Brother Maximus exclaimed, "You are of too proud a fpirit, you who dare to condemn divine works, and you are worthy of Hell-fire for your foolifh pride; inafmuch as Saint Francis in the day of yefterday performed fuch holy deeds, that had they been done by an Angel of God they could not have been more marvellous. Hence, if he command you to dafh yourfelf againft a rock, you fhould obey him and do fo; for thofe things which he has done upon this pilgrimage proceed from Divine Action, as is fet forth by the good refult which followed after them; forafmuch as if he had not pacified thofe who
ftrove

strove together, not only many bodies, as already there began to be seen, would have perished by the knife, but even also many souls would the Devil have dragged down into Hell; and yet you, vain and silly that you are, murmur at that which manifestly proceedeth from the will of God." And all these things which Brother Maximus spake within his own heart were straightway revealed of God to Saint Francis. Whence Saint Francis drawing near to him spake these words: " Abide by those things on which you now muse, forasmuch as they are good and useful, and inspired of God; but the first complaints which you uttered were blind and vain and arrogant, and instilled into your mind of the Devil." Then Brother Maximus saw clearly that Saint Francis knew the secrets of his heart, and knew for a surety that the Spirit of Divine Wisdom guided the Holy Father in his every action.

CHAPTER XII.

How Saint Francis beſtowed on Brother Maximus the Offices of Gate-Keeper, Almoner, and Cook: then at the Prayer of the other Brothers deprived him of them.

SAINT FRANCIS, wiſhing to mortify Brother Maximus, to the end that the many gifts and graces which God had given him might not make him Vainglorious, but that by virtue of Humility he might grow with them from virtue to virtue, upon a time when he dwelt in a ſolitary place with thoſe his firſt companions, very Saints, of whom was the ſaid Brother Maximus, ſpake one day to Brother Maximus before all his companions: "O Brother Maximus, all theſe your companions have the grace of contemplation and of prayer, but you have the grace to preach the word of God to the ſatisfaction of the people; and hence I deſire, to the end that they may apply themſelves to contemplation, that you do take upon yourſelf the offices of Door-keeper, of Almoner, and Cook. And when the other Brothers do eat, you ſhall eat without the convent

convent gate; to the end that thofe who come hither, before they knock you may fatisfy them with certain goodly words from God; fo that there be no need for any to iffue forth but only you; and this do through the fruits of holy obedience." Thereupon Brother Maximus drew on his cowl, and bowed his head, and humbly received and continued to obey this charge for many days, filling the offices of Door-keeper, of Almoner, and of Cook. Whence his Companions, like men illumined of God, began to feel great remorfe within their hearts, confidering that Brother Maximus was a man of exceeding great Perfectnefs, like unto themfelves or yet more, and upon him refted all the burden of the Convent and not on them. For the which thing they were all moved with one accord, and went in and prayed the Holy Father that it might pleafe him to diftribute thofe offices among them; forafmuch as their confciences could in no manner endure that Brother Maximus fhould undergo fuch toil. Hearing this, Saint Francis yielded to their counfels and confented to their wifh, and calling Brother Maximus, faid to him, "Brother Maximus, your companions defire to fhare in thofe
offices

offices which I have beſtowed upon you; and therefore I deſire that the ſaid offices may be divided." Brother Maximus ſaid with great Patience and Meekneſs, "Father, the burden which you lay upon me, be it all or but a part, I hold it as the work of God alone." Then Saint Francis, ſeeing the Loving-kindneſs of thoſe brothers and the humility of Brother Maximus, preached them a marvellous ſermon upon the moſt ſaintly quality of Humility; teaching them that the greater are the gifts and the graces beſtowed upon us by God, ſo much the more humble ſhould we be, foraſmuch as without Humility no virtue is acceptable in God's ſight. And the Sermon ended, he diſtributed the Offices with the utmoſt Affection.

CHAPTER XIII.

How Saint Francis and Brother Maximus laid the Bread which they had begged upon a Stone beside a Well, and Saint Francis loudly praised Poverty. Then He prayed unto God and Saint Peter and Saint Paul that they might enamour Him of divine Poverty; and how Saint Peter and Saint Paul appeared unto Him.

THAT wondrous servant and follower of Christ, which is Saint Francis, desiring to conform himself perfectly unto Christ in all things, who, as the Gospel tells us, sent out his Disciples two by two into all those cities and towns whither He was to go; therefore following the example of Christ he assembled together twelve Companions and sent them forth into the world to preach two by two. And to set them an example of true obedience, he first began to practise that which he did after preach. Hence having assigned to his Companions the other parts of the world, he, taking Brother Maximus as his companion, set forth towards the Province of France. And coming one day to a certain

certain town and being very hungry, they begged their bread as they went, according to the rule of their Order, for the love of God; and Saint Francis went through one quarter of the town and Brother Maximus through another. But forafmuch as Saint Francis was a man mean and low of ſtature, and hence was reputed a vile beggar by ſuch as knew him not, he only begged a few ſcanty cruſts and mouthfuls of dry bread; but to Brother Maximus, inaſmuch as he was great and well-favored, were given good pieces and large, and an abundance of bread, yea, whole loaves. Having begged, they met together without the town to eat, at a place where there was a clear well, and beſide it was a fair large ſtone, upon which each ſpread forth the alms which he had begged; and Saint Francis ſeeing that the pieces of bread begged by Brother Maximus were more and better and bigger than his own, rejoiced greatly, ſaying, "O Brother Maximus, we are not worthy of ſo great a treaſure;" and repeating theſe words many times, Brother Maximus replied, "Father, how can you talk of treaſures, where there is ſuch great poverty and ſuch lack of all things needful?
Here

Here is neither napkin nor knife, neither board nor trencher, neither houſe nor table, neither man-ſervant nor maid-ſervant." Saint Francis ſaid: "And this is that ſame which I repute a great treaſure, where nought is made ready by human induſtry; but all that is here is prepared by Divine Providence, as is plainly ſet forth in the bread which we have begged, in the table of fair ſtone, and in the well of clear water, and therefore I would that we ſhould pray to God that He teach us to love with all our heart the treaſure of Holy Poverty which is ſo noble a thing, and whoſe ſervant is God the Lord." And having ſaid theſe words, and having prayed, and having taken the bodily refection of thoſe cruſts of bread and of that water, they aroſe to journey into France; and coming to a church, Saint Francis ſaid to his Companion, "Let us enter into this church to pray." And ſtraightway Saint Francis retired behind the altar and fell to praying; and in that prayer he received exceeding fervor from the Divine Viſitation, which ſo inflamed his ſoul with the love of Holy Poverty, that what with the color of his face and with the yawning of his mouth he ſeemed to dart
forth

forth flames of love. And coming thus kindled unto his comrade, he ſaid, "Ah, ah, ah, Brother Maximus, give me thyſelf;" and theſe words he ſpake three times; and the third time Saint Francis lifted Brother Maximus in the air with his breath, and caſt him before him for the ſpace of a tall ſtaff; at which that ſame Brother Maximus was much amazed. He afterwards told his Companions that in that raiſing and impulſion of the breath, performed of Saint Francis, he felt ſuch ſpiritual ſweetneſs and conſolation of the Holy Ghoſt as he never before had known in his life. And this done, Saint Francis ſaid, "Comrade mine, let us go to Saint Peter and Saint Paul, and let us pray them that they will be pleaſed to teach us and aid us to poſſeſs the unbounded treaſure of moſt Holy Poverty; foraſmuch as it is a treaſure ſo worthy and ſo divine that we are not worthy to poſſeſs it in our moſt Vile Veſſels; ſeeing that it is that celeſtial virtue by which all things tranſitory and terreſtrial are trodden under foot, and by the which every care is ſmoothed from the Soul, to the end that it may freely be conjoined with the Everlaſting God; and this is that ſame virtue which
makes

makes the Soul ſtill bound to earth converſe with Angels in Heaven; and this it is which went with Chriſt even to the Croſs, was buried with Chriſt, roſe from the dead with Chriſt, with Chriſt aſcended into Heaven; which even in this life grants to Souls which truly love it the power to aſcend into Heaven, foraſmuch as it preſerves the armor of true Humility and Loving-kindneſs. And therefore let us pray the moſt Holy Apoſtles of Chriſt, who were perfect lovers of this Goſpel Pearl, that they will be pleaſed to beſtow on us this grace of our Lord Jeſus Chriſt, that of His moſt holy mercy He will make us worthy to be true lovers, followers, and humble diſciples of the moſt precious, moſt dearly beloved, and evangelical Poverty." And in ſuch diſcourſe they reached Rome, and entered into the Church of St. Peter; and Saint Francis began to pray in one corner of the Church and Brother Maximus in the other. And praying long with many tears and great devotion, the moſt Holy Apoſtles Peter and Paul appeared unto Saint Francis with great ſplendor, ſaying, "Foraſmuch as you demand and deſire to follow that which Chriſt and the Holy

Holy Apoſtles followed, the Lord Jeſus Chriſt ſends us to you to ſay that your prayer has been heard, and that God yields to you and to your followers the treaſure of moſt Holy Poverty in fulleſt meaſure. And alſo He bids us ſay unto you that whoſoever like you ſhall truly follow this deſire, he ſhall be bleſſed forevermore; and you and all your companions ſhall be bleſſed of God." And having uttered theſe words they vaniſhed away, leaving Saint Francis greatly conſoled. The ſame roſe from his prayers and returned to his Companion and aſked him if God had revealed nothing to him. And he anſwered, "No." Then Saint Francis told him how the Holy Apoſtles had appeared unto him, and that which they had revealed to him. Upon which, each being filled with joy, they determined to return into the Vale of Spoleto, journeying not into France.

CHAPTER XIV.

How Saint Francis, discoursing of God with his Brethren, He appeared in their Midst.

SAINT FRANCIS, in the early days of the foundation of his Order, being gathered together with his Companions, discoursing of Christ, in the ardor of his spirit, did charge one among them that he open his mouth in the name of God, and speak concerning God that which the Holy Ghost should inspire him to say. The Brother obeying the command, and speaking marvellous well concerning God, Saint Francis imposed silence upon him, and required the same of another friar. He obeying, and speaking subtilely of God, Saint Francis likewise imposed silence upon him; and he commanded a third that he should speak of God, who likewise began to talk so wisely of the secret things of God that Saint Francis knew certainly that he, as also the other two, spake from the Holy Ghost, and this also was proven by an example, and by an express sign; for they being in this discourse, Christ the Blessed appeared

appeared in their midſt viſibly and in the bodily form of a moſt lovely Youth; and bleſſing them, he filled them all with ſuch grace and ſweetneſs that they were raviſhed out of themſelves, and fell like dead men, knowing nought of this world. And then returning to their ſenſes, Saint Francis ſaid to them: "My beloved Brothers, give thanks to God, Who has been pleaſed to reveal the treaſures of the Divine Wiſdom through the mouths of the ſimple; foraſmuch as it is God Who opes the mouth of the dumb and makes the tongue of the ſimple to diſcourſe moſt wiſely."

CHAPTER XV.

How Saint Clara ate with Saint Francis and with his Brother Monks in St. Mary of the Angels.

SAINT FRANCIS, when he was at Aſſiſi, ofttimes viſited Saint Clara, giving her holy teachings; and ſhe having the greateſt deſire to eat with him but once, and entreating him many times to this end, he would never grant her that Conſolation. Hence,

Hence his Companions, seeing the desire of Saint Clara, said to Saint Francis: "Father, to us it seems that such severity is not in accordance with Divine Charity, that Sister Clara, a virgin so saintly and so beloved of God, should not find favor in your sight to gain so small a thing as to eat with you; and especially considering that she through your preachings forsook riches and all the pomps of this world; and verily, were she to ask you a much greater grace than this, you should grant it to your spiritual child." Then Saint Francis replied, "Does it seem to you that I should hear her prayer?" His Companions answered, "Father, yes; it is a righteous thing that you should grant her request, and a consolation." Then Saint Francis said: "Since it seems meet to you, it seems so also unto me. But that she may be the more consoled, I desire that this meal should be eaten in the Church of St. Mary of the Angels, forasmuch as she has long been cloistered in St. Damian: therefore it will rejoice her much to see the Church of St. Mary, where her locks were shorn off and she was made the bride of Jesus Christ; and there we will eat together in the name of God." When the day

day came appointed for this, Saint Clara left her Convent with one companion, accompanied by the Companions of Saint Francis, and came to St. Mary of the Angels; and having devoutly faluted the Virgin Mary before the altar, where her locks had been fhorn and the veil had been placed upon her head, they led her about to fee the place until at laft it was time to dine. And Saint Francis ordered the cloth to be laid in their midft upon the bare ground, as he was wont to do. And when the hour for dinner came, Saint Francis and Saint Clara fat down together, and one of the Comrades of Saint Francis with Saint Clara's Companion, and then all their other Companions took their places humbly. And for the firft difh Saint Francis began to talk of God fo fweetly, fo nobly, fo wondrous well, that the abundance of the Divine grace defcending upon them, they were all tranfported as it were to Heaven. And being thus tranfported, with eyes and hands raifed to Heaven, the men of Affifi and of Bettona, and of the country round about, faw how St. Mary of the Angels, and all that place, and the wood which ftood befide it, burned fiercely; and it feemed

seemed as it were a great fire, which filled the Church, and the place, and the wood also; wherefore the people of Assisi in great haste ran thither to put out the Fire, truly thinking that everything was burning. But on reaching the spot, and finding no flames, they entered in, and found Saint Francis with Saint Clara, and with all their companions, absorbed in the contemplation of God, and sitting around that humble board. Whence they perceived that those were divine and not material flames, which God had caused to appear miraculously, to show forth and signify the Fire of the Divine Love with which the souls of those holy monks and nuns were consumed; wherefore they departed with great Consolation in their hearts, and with holy Edification. Then after a great space Saint Francis returning to himself, and likewise Saint Clara, together with the others, and feeling themselves much comforted by the spiritual food, they cared little for bodily sustenance. And thus, this blessed meal being ended, Saint Clara, well escorted, returned to St. Damian; whence her Sisters, seeing her coming, rejoiced greatly, inasmuch as they feared lest Saint Francis had sent her to rule
over

over some other convent, even as he had already sent Sister Agnes, her ghostly sister, as abbess to rule over the monastery of Monticelli at Florence; and Saint Francis had once said to Saint Clara, "Be ready, if I need you, that I may send you somewhither," and she, as beseemed a daughter of Holy Obedience, had made answer, "Father, I am ever ready to go whithersoever you may send me." And hence the Sisters rejoiced greatly when they saw her again among them: and Saint Clara thenceforth remained much consoled.

CHAPTER XVI.

How Saint Francis received the Advice of Saint Clara and of Holy Brother Sylvester, that he should go forth and preach, converting the People; and he created the Third Order, and preached to the Birds and silenced the young Swallows.

THAT humble servant of Jesus Christ, Saint Francis, shortly after his conversion, having already gathered together many companions and received them into
the

the Order, fell into deep thought and into grave doubt as to what he fhould do,—whether he fhould devote himfelf wholly to prayer, or whether indeed he fhould fometimes preach; and on this fubject he greatly defired to know the will of God. And forafmuch as the Saintly Humility which was in him would not let him truft to himfelf or to his own prayers alone, he ftrove to feek out the Divine will through the prayers of others; hence he called Brother Maximus, and fpake to him thus: "Go to Sifter Clara and tell her from me that fhe, with certain of her moft fpiritual companions, fhall pray devoutly to God that it may pleafe Him to reveal to me whether it is better that I fhould devote myfelf to preaching, or merely to prayer. And then go to Brother Sylvefter and fay the fame words." This was that fame Mafter Sylvefter who had feen a golden crofs come forth from the mouth of Saint Francis, which was as high as the heavens and as broad as the confines of the globe. And fuch were the devotion and the fanctity of this fame Brother Sylvefter, that whatfoever he afked of God, even that fame he obtained, and his prayer was granted, and many

many times he ſpake with God; and yet Saint Francis alſo had great piety. Brother Maximus went forth, and according to the command of Saint Francis he fulfilled his errand firſt to Saint Clara and then to Brother Sylveſter; who, when he had received it, incontinently fell to praying, and praying he heard the Divine voice, and turning to Brother Maximus he ſaid: "Thus ſaith the Lord, which you ſhall repeat to Brother Francis,—that God did not call him unto this ſtate for himſelf alone, but that he might reap a harveſt of ſouls, and many through him ſhall be ſaved." Having this anſwer, Brother Maximus returned to Saint Clara to know that which ſhe had obtained of God. And ſhe made anſwer that ſhe and her Companions had had from God the ſelfsame anſwer which Brother Sylveſter had had. With this Brother Maximus returned to Saint Francis; and Saint Francis received him with the utmoſt Affection, waſhing his feet and laying the cloth for him to dine. And after eating, Saint Francis called Brother Maximus into the thick wood; and there he knelt before him, and drawing down his Cowl over his face, he croſſed his arms and aſked

asked him, saying, "What does my Lord and Master Jesus Christ command me to do?" Brother Maximus made answer: "Both to Brother Sylvester and to Sister Clara, with her Sisters, Christ has replied and made manifest that it is His will that you shall go forth into the world to preach; forasmuch as He did not call you for yourself alone, but even also for the salvation of others." And then Saint Francis, when that he had heard this answer and learned therefrom the will of Jesus Christ, rose up with the greatest fervor, saying, "Let us go forth in the name of God." And he took for his Companions Brother Maximus and Brother Andrew, holy men both; and going forth filled with the things of the Spirit, without considering their road or their way, they came to a Castle, which is called Savurniano, and Saint Francis began to preach; and he first commanded the Swallows, which were singing, to keep silence so long as until he should have preached; and the Swallows obeyed him; and he preached in this place with such fervor that all the men and the women in that Castle, from devotion, would have followed after him and forsaken the Castle; but Saint Francis forbade them, saying,

ſaying, "Be not in haſte, and depart not, and I will order all things which you are to do for the ſalvation of your ſoul." And then he created the Third Order, for the Univerſal Salvation of all men; and thus leaving many conſoled and well difpoſed to penitence, he departed from thence and came to Cannajo and Bevagno. And paſſing on his way with the ſelfſame fervor, he raiſed his eyes and ſaw certain trees by the roadſide in which were an infinite multitude of birds; at which Saint Francis marvelled greatly, and ſaid to his Companions, "Await me here in the road, and I will go and preach to my Siſters the birds." And he entered the field and began to preach to the birds which were on the ground; and ſuddenly thoſe which were in the trees came down to him, and as many as there were they all ſtood quietly until Saint Francis had done preaching; and even then they did not depart until ſuch time as he had given them his bleſſing; and according to the later recital of Brother Maximus to Brother James of Maſſa, Saint Francis moving among them touched them with his cape, but not one moved. The ſubſtance of Saint Francis' ſermon was this: "My Siſters the birds,

birds, ye are greatly beholden unto God your Creator, and always and in every place it is your duty to praife Him, forafmuch as He hath given you freedom to fly in every place; alfo hath He given you raiment twofold and threefold almoft, becaufe He preferved your Seed in the ark of Noah, that your race might never be lefs. Again, ye are bounden to Him for the element of the air, which He has deputed unto you; moreover, you fow not, neither do you reap, and God feeds you, and gives you the ftreams and fountains for your thirft; He gives you mountains and valleys for your refuge; tall trees wherein to make your nefts; and inafmuch as you neither fpin nor weave, God clothes you, you and your children; hence ye fhould love your Creator greatly, Who gives you fuch great benefits, and therefore beware, my Sifters, of the fin of ingratitude, and ever ftrive to praife God." Saint Francis faying thefe words to them, all thofe birds, as many as there were, began to ope their beaks and ftretch forth their necks and fpread their wings and reverently to bow their heads even to the earth, and by their acts and their fongs to fet forth that the Holy Father gave them
the

SAINT FRANCIS PREACHING TO THE BIRDS.

From the Painting by Giotto.

the utmoſt delight; and Saint Francis rejoiced with them, pleaſed and marvelling much to ſee ſo vaſt a multitude of birds, and their moſt beautiful variety, their attention and familiarity; for the which things in them he devoutly praiſed the Creator. Finally, his preaching ended, Saint Francis made them the ſign of the Croſs and gave them leave to depart; and then all thoſe birds roſe into the air with wondrous ſongs; and then, according to the Croſs which Saint Francis had made them, they divided into four parts; and the one part flew towards the eaſt, and the other towards the weſt, and the one part towards the ſouth, and the other towards the north, and each band went away ſinging marvellous ſongs; ſignifying by this how that Saint Francis, the Enſign of the Croſs of Chriſt, had come to preach to them, and had made the ſign of the Croſs over them, according to which they had ſcattered to the four quarters of the globe. Thus the preaching of the Croſs of Chriſt renewed by Saint Francis was by him and his Brethren borne throughout the whole world; which Brethren, even as the birds, poſſeſſed nothing of this world's goods, but committed their life to the ſole and only providence of God.

CHAPTER XVII.

How a Francifcan Child, while Saint Francis prayed by Night, faw Chrift and the Virgin Mary, and many other Saints with Him.

A VERY pure and innocent child was received into the Order while Saint Francis yet lived; and he abode in a fmall convent, wherein from fheer neceffity the Brethren flept in caft-off rags. Saint Francis coming on a time to this place, at eventide, Complines being faid, he went to fleep betimes, to the end that he might rife in the night to pray when the other Brothers flept, as was his wont. The faid child determined folicitoufly to watch the ways of Saint Francis, for the better acquaintance with his fanctity, and efpecially to know that which he did at night when he arofe from bed. And to the end that fleep might not overtake him, this little lad lay down to fleep by the fide of Saint Francis, and bound his girdle to that of Saint Francis, that he might have warning if he rofe up: and of this Saint Francis knew not aught. But in the firft fleep of night, when all the other

other Brothers flumbered, he arofe and found his girdle thus bound, and loofed it pioufly, fo that the child was not awakened; and Saint Francis ftraightway went out into the Wood, which was hard by that place, and entered into a tiny cell which was there and fell to praying. And after a certain fpace the child awoke, and finding the girdle loofed and Saint Francis arifen, he alfo rofe up and went about feeking him; and finding the door open whence he had iffued forth into the Wood, he imagined that Saint Francis had gone thither, and he alfo followed after into the Wood. And having drawn near to the fpot where Saint Francis was at prayer, he began to hear the murmur of many voices; and drawing ever nearer to fee and to underftand that which he heard, he beheld a great and wondrous light which fhone round about Saint Francis, and therein he faw Chrift, and the Virgin Mary, and Saint John the Baptift, and Saint John the Evangelift, and a vaft multitude of Angels, who difcourfed with Saint Francis. Seeing and hearing thefe things, the child fell to the earth in a fwoon; then, the Myftery of this holy apparition completed, and Saint Francis

Francis being about to return to the convent, he found the child with his foot, — which is to fay, he ftumbled over him, — lying like one dead; and from compaffion he lifted him up and took him in his arms, as the good Shepherd does his fheep. And then learning from him how that he had feen that felfsame vifion, he commanded him never to fpeak of it to living man, that is, fo long as he himfelf fhould yet live. The child, growing in the grace of God and the favor of Saint Francis, became a valiant member of the Order; and he, after the death of Saint Francis, revealed the faid vifion to the Brethren.

CHAPTER XVIII.

Of the marvellous Chapter held by Saint Francis in the Church of St. Mary of the Angels, where were affembled more than five thoufand of the Brethren.

FRANCIS, faithful fervant of Chrift, upon a time held a General Chapter at St. Mary of the Angels, at which fame Chapter were affembled more than five thoufand thouſand of the Brethren; and there came thither Saint Dominic, the head and very foundation of the Order of Preaching or Dominican Friars, who was then journeying from Burgundy to Rome. And hearing of the congregation of the Chapter which Saint Francis had called together upon the plain round about St. Mary of the Angels, he turned aſide to ſee it, with ſeven Brothers of his Order. There was furthermore at this Chapter a Cardinal moſt piouſly attached to Saint Francis, to whom he had propheſied that he ſhould yet be Pope, and even ſo it was; the which Cardinal had come expreſſly from Perugia, where the Court abode, to Aſſiſi; daily he came to viſit Saint Francis and his Brothers, and daily he ſang the Maſs, and daily he preached a ſermon to the Brethren in the Chapter; and the ſaid Cardinal felt the utmoſt devotion and delight when he came to viſit that holy College. And ſeeing the Brethren ſitting round about St. Mary's, rank on rank, here forty, here an hundred, and here eighty together, all abſorbed in diſcourſing of God, in Prayers and Lamentation, in acts of Charity, and they obſerving ſuch ſilence, and

and ſo great their modeſty that no fainteſt noiſe nor clamor was to be heard, and marvelling at ſo orderly and ſo vaſt a multitude, with tears and much devotion he ſaid, " Verily, verily this is the Encampment and the Army of the Knights of God." In all that multitude no man was heard recounting idle tales nor Jeſts; but wherever a band of Brothers was met together, either they prayed, or they read their Offices, or they bewailed their ſins or thoſe of their benefactors, or they diſcourſed of the Salvation of their ſouls. Upon that field were huts woven of hurdles or of reeds, divided into bands according to the Friars from various provinces; and hence that Chapter was called the Chapter of the Hurdles and alſo of the Reeds. Their beds were the bare ground, and ſome among them had a little ſtraw; their Pillows were of ſtone or of wood; by reaſon of which all who heard or ſaw them felt much Admiration for their devotion. And ſo great was the fame of their Sanctity, that there came thither from the Papal Court, which was then at Perugia, and from other parts of the Vale of Spoleto, many counts, barons, cavaliers, and other gentlemen, and many country people and

and Cardinals and Biſhops and Abbots with many other of the clergy to ſee a congregation ſo holy, ſo vaſt, and yet ſo humble, for never before ſince the world began had ſo many holy men been met together; and chiefly they came to ſee the Head and moſt Holy Father of theſe ſaintly folk, which had robbed the world of ſo fair a prey, and gathered together ſo beauteous and ſo devout a flock to follow in the footſteps of the true Shepherd Chriſt Jeſus. The entire General Chapter being then aſſembled, the Holy Father and Commander of all, Saint Francis, with fervent ſpirit ſet forth the Word of God, and preached to them in a loud voice the words which the Holy Ghoſt put into his mouth; and as the ſubject of his ſermon he ſpake theſe words: "My ſons, great things have we promiſed unto God: far greater are promiſed to us of God, if we keep our promiſes unto Him: and we may ſurely await thoſe which are promiſed unto us. Brief are the pleaſures of this World; the pains that follow in their train are everlaſting; ſlight are the Pangs of this life, but the Glory of the other life is infinite." And preaching devoutly upon this text, he
comforted

comforted and perfuaded the Brothers to obedience and reverence for their Holy Mother Church, and to brotherly affection, and to worfhip God before all the people, to be patient in worldly Adverfity, and temperate in Profperity, to obferve Purity and angelic Chaftity, and to preferve peace and concord with God and with man and with their own confcience, and to love and purfue the moft Holy Poverty. And upon this point he fpake thefe words: "I charge you, by the fruits of your holy vow of obedience, that all ye, who are gathered together here, take no thought to yourfelves, nor any heed for what ye fhall eat, or fhall drink, or wherewithal ye fhall be clothed, but apply yourfelves only to praying and praifing God; and leave all care for your bodies unto Him, forafmuch as He hath a fpecial care over you." And every man among them, as many as there were there, received this command with a light heart and a cheerful face; and Saint Francis having ended his fermon, they all fell to praying. At which Saint Dominic, who was prefent at thefe things, marvelled greatly at the charge of Saint Francis, and held him to be indifcreet, being unable to fancy how fo vaft a hoft hoſt could exiſt without taking any thought or heed for the things of the Body. But the great Shepherd Chriſt the bleſt, deſiring to ſhow how He cares for His Sheep and His ſingular love for His poor followers, ſtraightway inſpired the men of Perugia, of Spoleto, of Fuligno, of Spello, Aſſiſi, and the other regions round about, to bear food and drink to that holy congregation. And lo ſuddenly a great multitude of men came forth from the ſaid regions, with beaſts of burden, horſes, and carts, laden with bread and wine, with honeycomb and with cheeſe, and with other good things to eat, according as Chriſt's poor had need. Moreover they bore alſo napkins, jugs, bowls, glaſſes, and other veſſels, enough to ſerve ſo vaſt a multitude: and he counted himſelf happy who could ſet forth moſt offerings or could moſt acceptably ſerve; ininaſmuch as even the Knights and Barons and other Gentlemen, who came thither to ſee, ſerved before them with great humility and devotion. Wherefore Saint Dominic, ſeeing theſe things, and knowing truly that a Divine Providence did work within them, humbly acknowledged that he had falſely judged Saint Francis as indiſcreet in his commands;

commands; and going before him, he knelt down and humbly confeſſed his guilt, and added: "Verily God hath an eſpecial care for theſe poor ſaints, and I knew it not; and from this time forth I promiſe to obſerve the Holy Poverty of the Goſpels, and I curſe in the name of God all thoſe Brethren of my Order who ſhall within that ſame Order preſume to hold property." Thus Saint Dominic was much edified by the faith of the moſt holy Francis, and by the obedience to their vow of poverty diſplayed by ſo vaſt and orderly a community, and by the Divine Providence and the copious abundance of every good thing. At that ſame Chapter ſome ſaid to Saint Francis that many of the Friars wore inſtruments of torture next their ſkin, for the which thing many fell ill, and hence died, and many were thus prevented from prayer. At which Saint Francis, like a moſt prudent Father, by his vow of Holy Obedience charged every man who might wear ſuch inſtruments of torture, to ſtrip them off and lay them before him, and ſo it was done; and they reckoned at leaſt five hundred of one kind; and ſo many were there of iron rings taken from arms and breaſt, that

that they formed a little mountain; and Saint Francis left them where they lay. Then, the Chapter being ended, Saint Francis comforted them all mightily, and inſtructed them how they might live without ſin in this wicked world, and ſent them all home, every man to his own Province, with the bleſſing of God, all greatly conſoled and full of ſpiritual joy.

CHAPTER XIX.

How the Grapes in the Vineyard of the Prieſt of Rieti, in whoſe Houſe Saint Francis prayed, were trampled and plucked by the many People which came thither to him; and then miraculouſly made more Wine than ever before, even as Saint Francis had promiſed. And how the Lord revealed to Saint Francis that Paradiſe ſhould be his lot.

SAINT FRANCIS being once afflicted with a grievous malady of the eyes, Cardinal Ugolino, Protector of the Order, for the great love he bore him, wrote to him bidding him come to him at Rieti, where were moſt excellent doctors for the eyes. Then Saint Francis, having received

ceived the Cardinal's letter, set forth first to Saint Damian's, where dwelt Saint Clara, that most faithful spouse of Christ, to give her some little consolation, and thence to journey to the Cardinal. Being there, the next night Saint Francis found his eyes so much worse that he could see no ray of light; hence being unable to depart, Saint Clara made him a little cell of reeds wherein he might better rest. But Saint Francis, what with the anguish of his eyes, and what with the multitude of rats and mice which did disturb him mightily, could find no Peace, neither by day nor by night. And enduring long these pangs and tribulations, he began to think and to see that this was a scourge sent by God to punish him for his sins; and he began to thank the Lord with his whole heart and with his lips, and then he cried out in a loud voice and said: "My Lord, worthy am I of this and of far worse. My Lord Jesus Christ, the Good Shepherd, who hast shown Thy mercy to sinners by various bodily pains and agonies, grant me, Thy rebellious sheep, grace and power to hold to Thee through all illness, anguish, and pain." And in the midst of this prayer he heard

heard a voice from Heaven, saying, "Francis, answer me: Were all the earth gold, and all the seas and springs and streams precious balm, and all the mountains and hills and rocks precious stones, and you should find another treasure as much more noble than these things as gold is more noble than earth, and balm than clear water, and precious stones than rocks and hills, and with this your affliction you were given that far nobler treasure, should you not then be content indeed and happy of heart?" Saint Francis made answer, saying, "Lord, I am not worthy of such a precious treasure;" and the voice of God said unto him, "Rejoice, Francis, and be exceeding glad, for this is the treasure of Life Eternal, which I reserved for you, and with which from this time forth I invest you; and this your infirmity and affliction is but the pledge and token of that Blessed Treasure." Then Saint Francis called his Companion, with exceeding great joy at so glorious a promise, and said, "Let us set forth to the Cardinal;" and comforting first Saint Clara with holy words, and she humbly taking leave of them, he took his way towards Rieti. And when he had drawn
near

near, so vast a multitude of people came forth to meet him, that he could not therefore enter into the city; but he went to a Church, which was distant perhaps two miles from the town. The citizens, knowing that he was within that Church, ran thither in such numbers to behold him, that the vineyard of the said Church was laid waste, and the grapes were all gathered; at which the Priest was greatly grieved within himself, and repented that he had received Saint Francis. The Priest's thought being revealed of God to Saint Francis, he called him before him, saying: "Beloved Father, how many measures of wine does your vineyard yield you in the best of years?" He answered, "Twelve measures." Saint Francis said: "I pray you, Father, patiently to permit me to abide with you yet a few days, forasmuch as I find much rest here, and suffer every man to pluck the grapes of this your vineyard, for the love of God, and of me a poor beggar; and I promise you in the name of my Master Christ Jesus, that it shall yield you every year twenty measures." And this did Saint Francis to the end that he might sojourn there, where he he reaped a rich harveſt of ſouls, from the multitude that came thither; many of whom departed thence drunk with Divine Love, and forſook the world. The Prieſt had faith in the promiſe of Saint Francis, and freely ſuffered all who came to pluck the grapes. Wonderful to relate! The vineyard was laid waſte and bare ſo that ſcarce a cluſter of grapes remained upon the vine. The time for the vintage came, and the Prieſt gathered in thoſe ſcanty cluſters, and placed them in the preſs and trod them out, and according to the promiſe of Saint Francis they yielded him twenty meaſures of the beſt wine. By which miracle is manifeſtly ſet forth, that as by the merits of Saint Francis the vine ſtripped of its grapes yet abounded in wine, ſo the Chriſtian people, made bare of virtues by their ſins, through the merits and doctrine of Saint Francis ofttimes abound in the good fruits of repentance.

CHAPTER XX.

Of a very fair Vision, seen by a young Friar, who held the Cowl in such abomination that He was disposed to lay aside his Habit and forsake the Order.

A CERTAIN very noble and delicate youth entered the Order of Saint Francis; the which after the space of some days, by the instigation of the Devil, began to hold the Habit which he wore in such abomination, that he seemed to wear the vilest sackcloth; he had a loathing for the sleeves, he abhorred the cowl, and its length and harshness seemed to him an unbearable burden. And his distaste for the Religious Life ever increasing, he at last proposed to give up the Habit and return to the world. It had become his custom, according as he had been taught by his master, to kneel most reverently at whatsoever hour he might pass before the altar of the Convent whereon the Body of Christ was kept, and drawing his cowl over his head, to bow low with crossed arms. It happened, that upon the selfsame night wherein

wherein he was to depart and go forth from the Order, he was forced to paſs before the Convent Altar; and paſſing, as was his wont, he knelt and made a humble reverence. And ſuddenly he was rapt in an ecſtaſy, and was ſhown by God a wondrous Viſion, foraſmuch as he ſaw before him an almoſt infinite number of ſaints, walking as in proceſſion, two by two, arrayed in moſt fair and precious robes of linen, and their faces and their hands ſhone like the ſun, and they paſſed along with angelic ſongs and ſounds; among which ſaints were two more nobly clad and adorned than all the others, and they were ſet round about with ſuch luſtre that all who gazed upon them were filled with exceeding great Awe; and almoſt at the end of the proceſſion he ſaw one decked with ſuch glory that he ſeemed a new-made knight, more honored than the reſt. This youth beholding the ſaid viſion, marvelled and knew not what this proceſſion was meant to ſignify, and he ventured not to aſk any man, but remained ſtruck dumb with the delight of it. And neverthelefs all the proceſſion having paſſed him by, he plucked up his ſpirits and ran forthwith to the

the laſt men in it; and with great dread, he aſked them, ſaying: "Oh, my Beloved, I pray you that it may pleaſe you to tell me who are theſe wondrous beings, which ſeem ſo glorious in this proceſſion?" And they made anſwer: "Know, O ſon, that we are all Gray Friars, who come hither from the ſplendors of Paradiſe." And he again queſtioned them, ſaying: "Who are yonder two, who ſhine yet more radiant than the reſt?" They made anſwer: "Thoſe are Saint Francis and Saint Antony; and that laſt, whom you ſee ſo greatly honored, is a Holy Brother who died but newly; who, foraſmuch as he fought valiantly againſt all temptation, and perſevered unto the end, we conduct in triumph to the glories of Paradiſe; and theſe garments of fair linen, wherewith we are arrayed, are given us of God in exchange for the coarſe tunics which patiently we wore in the Religious Order; and the glorious luſtre which you ſee round about us is given us of God for the Humility and Patience and for the Holy Poverty and Obedience and Chaſtity which we obſerved unto the end. And therefore, ſon, hold it not hard to bear the ſackcloth of Religion which

is

is ſo fruitful of reward; foraſmuch, as if with the ſackcloth of Saint Francis, for love of Chriſt, you deſpiſe the world, and mortify the fleſh, and fight a good fight againſt the Foul Fiend, you ſhall have raiment like unto that which we do wear, and a glory of light." And having heard theſe words, the youth returned to his ſenſes, and greatly comforted by the viſion, he drove far from him all temptation, and confeſſed his ſin before his Superior and the Brethren; and from that time forth he ardently longed for aſperity of penitence and of attire, and ended his life in the Order in great holineſs.

CHAPTER XXI.

Of the Moſt Holy Miracle, which Saint Francis performed, when he converted the very fierce Wolf at Gubbio.

IN the days when Saint Francis dwelt in the city of Gubbio, there appeared in that region a very great, terrible, and fierce Wolf, the which not only devoured animals, but even alſo men; inſomuch that all the citizens

citizens of that place ſtood in great dread of him; foraſmuch as many times he came very near to the town; and nevertheleſs none who chanced to meet with him alone could in any wiſe defend himſelf againſt him. And ſo great was the fear of this Wolf, that none ventured forth into the country. Wherefore Saint Francis, having compaſ- ſion upon the men of that land, deſired to go forth unto this Wolf,—albeit the citi- zens, every man among them, counſelled him againſt it,—and making the ſign of the Moſt Holy Croſs, he ſet forth into the country round about, he with his Companions, put- ting all his truſt in God. And the others doubting whether they ſhould go farther, Saint Francis took his way towards the place where the Wolf lay. And lo, ſeeing ſo many citizens, who had come forth to ſee ſuch a miracle, the ſaid Wolf came out to meet Saint Francis with open mouth; and drawing near to him, Saint Francis made the ſign of the Moſt Holy Croſs, and called unto him, ſaying: "Come hither, Brother Wolf; I command you in the name of Chriſt Jeſus, that you do no manner of evil either to me or to any other man." Wonderful to relate! Immediately that
Saint

Saint Francis made the sign of the Crofs, the terrible Wolf clofed his jaws and gave over running; and hearing this command, he came meekly as any lamb, and laid himfelf down at the feet of Saint Francis. And thereupon Saint Francis addreffed him in thefe words, faying: "Brother Wolf, you do much harm in thefe parts, and you have done great evil, killing and devouring God's creatures without His fovereign leave. And not only have you killed and devoured beafts, but you have dared to kill men, made in the image of God; for the which thing you are worthy of the gallows, like any thief and villanous murderer; and all the people cry out and murmur againft you, and all the land is hoftile unto you. But I defire, Brother Wolf, to make peace between you and them, fo that you may offend no more, and they fhall forgive you all your paft offences, and neither men nor dogs fhall purfue you any more." Having uttered thefe words, the Wolf by the motions of his body and his tail and his eyes, and by bowing his head, fet forth that he accepted that which Saint Francis faid, and defired to obferve it. Then Saint Francis began again: "Brother Wolf, inafmuch as it pleafes

pleases you to make and to keep this peace, I promise you that I will see to it that your living shall be given you continually, so long as you shall live, by the men of this country, so that you shall not suffer hunger; forasmuch as I am well aware that hunger has caused your every crime. But since I get for you this grace, I require, Brother Wolf, your promise never again to do harm to any human being, neither to any beast. Do you promise?" And the Wolf, by bowing his head, plainly gave sign that he promised. And Saint Francis said farther: "Brother Wolf, I desire you to give me some token of this your promise, although I have full faith in your loyalty." And Saint Francis stretching forth his hand, the Wolf lifted up his right paw and confidingly laid it in the hand of Saint Francis, giving him this pledge of his faith, as best he could. And then Saint Francis said: "Brother Wolf, I charge you in the name of Christ Jesus that you now follow me, nothing doubting, and we will go forth and conclude this peace in God's name." And the Wolf obediently followed after him, like any lamb; so that the citizens, seeing this, marvelled greatly. And suddenly the news was
spread

spread throughout all the city: so that the people, men as well as women, great as well as small, young as well as old, flocked to the market-place to behold the Wolf with Saint Francis. And all the people being gathered together, Saint Francis rose up and began to preach to them, saying among other things: "Inasmuch as for your sins, God hath permitted certain evil things and sundry pestilences; and far more dangerous as are the flames of Hell, which endure eternally for the damned, than is the wrath of the Wolf, which can but kill the body, — so much more therefore should ye fear the jaws of Hell, when the mouth of one small animal can terrify and alarm so vast a multitude! Turn then, my Beloved, unto God, and repent worthily of your sins, and God shall rid you of the Wolf in this present time, and of the fires of Hell in time to come." And having preached, Saint Francis said: "Hearken, my Brethren: Brother Wolf, who stands here before you, hath promised and given me a token of his good faith to make peace with you, and never to offend you more in anything whatsoever; and you must promise henceforth to give him daily all that is needful to him, and I will be bailſman for him, that he will firmly hold to his compact of peace." Then all the people with one accord promiſed to feed him continually. And Saint Francis, before them all, ſaid to the Wolf: "And you, Brother Wolf, do you promiſe to keep the peace with theſe people, and to offend no more againſt men, neither againſt beaſts, nor any other creatures?" And the Wolf knelt before him, and bowed his head, and with ſubmiſſive motions of body and tail and ears ſhowed in ſo far as he was able, that he would keep his every promiſe. Saint Francis ſaid: "Brother Wolf, I deſire that even as you gave me a pledge of this your promiſe outſide the gates, ſo here before all theſe people you ſhall give me a token of your good faith, and that you will not cheat me of my promiſe and ſecurity which I have given for you." Then the Wolf, lifting up his right paw, laid it in the hand of Saint Francis. Upon this action and upon thoſe which had gone before, there was ſuch rejoicing and ſuch marvelling in all the people, both at the devotion of the Saint, and at the novelty of the miracle, and at the peace with the Wolf, that all began to cry aloud unto Heaven, praiſing

praising and blessing God, that had sent unto them Saint Francis, who by his great merits had freed them from the mouth of this cruel beast. And then the said Wolf lived two years in Gubbio, and entered meekly into every house, going from door to door, doing no manner of mischief to any man, and none being done to him. And he was courteously nourished by the people; and roaming thus through the land and from house to house, never any dog barked at his coming in or at his going out. Finally, after two years, Brother Wolf died of old age; at the which the citizens mourned much, inasmuch as seeing him moving so meekly through the city, they were the more mindful of the virtue and sanctity of Saint Francis.

CHAPTER XXII.

How Saint Francis tamed the wild Turtle-Doves.

A BOY one day took a number of turtle-doves, and carrying them to the market-place for sale, he met Saint Francis, who ever felt singular compassion for all

all gentle animals. Gazing at these turtle-doves with pitiful eyes, he said to the boy: "Oh, good youth, give them to me, I pray you; nor suffer birds so meek and gentle, to whom chaste, humble, and faithful souls are likened in the Scriptures, to fall into the hands of cruel men, who will slay them." The boy, suddenly inspired of God, gave them all to Saint Francis; and he receiving them in his bosom, began to speak sweetly unto them: "O my Sisters, simple, chaste, and innocent doves, why did ye suffer yourselves to be taken? I would now rescue you from death, and make nests for you, that ye may increase and bring forth young, according to the command of the Lord our God." And Saint Francis went forth, and made nests for every one; and they, using them, began to lay eggs, and to bring forth young before the Friars; "and so tame were they and consorted so freely with Saint Francis and the other Friars," as they had been hens and ever fed from their hands, and departed not from among them, until Saint Francis with his blessing gave them leave to fly thence. And to the boy who gave them to him Saint Francis said: "Son, you shall yet be a brother in this Order, and ſhall ſerve Chriſt Jeſus worthily," and ſo it was; foraſmuch as the boy became a friar and lived in the Order with great ſanctity.

CHAPTER XXIII.

How Saint Francis ſet free the Friar who had ſinned with the aid of the Devil.

SAINT FRANCIS, being once at prayer within the Convent of Portiuncula, beheld by Divine Revelation all that Convent ſurrounded and beſieged of Demons, after the manner of an huge army; but none among them could enter into the Convent, foraſmuch as thoſe friars were of ſuch ſanctity, that the Demons found no man among them into whom they might enter. But perſevering thus, upon a certain day, one of thoſe ſame friars grew angry with another one, and took counſel with his own heart, how he might accuſe him and take vengeance upon him; for the which thing, he cheriſhing thus this evil thought, the Demon, finding the door open, entered in and placed himſelf upon the neck of that ſame

same friar. The pious and careful Shepherd, who watcheth ever over his flocks, seeing therefore that the Wolf had entered in to devour his Sheep, suddenly summoned that friar before him, and charged him that he should forthwith confess the Poison of Hate conceived of him against his neighbor, whereby he had fallen into the hands of the Enemy. Upon which he, frighted to feel himself read of the Holy Father, straightway made known all his venom and rancor, and revealed his guilt, and humbly begged for justice tempered with mercy; and this done, being absolved from his sin, and having received his punishment, suddenly, before the face of Saint Francis, the Demon departed thence; and the friar thus set free from the hands of the cruel Beast, through the kindness of the good Shepherd, gave thanks unto God: and returning chastened and corrected to the flock of the Holy Shepherd, thenceforth lived in great sanctity.

CHAPTER XXIV.

How Saint Francis converted the Sultan of Babylon to the Faith.

SAINT FRANCIS, led by zeal for the faith of Chriſt and by his longing for martyrdom, went upon a time acroſs the ſeas with twelve of his moſt Holy Companions, bent upon going ſtraight to the Sultan of Babylon; and coming into a region of Saracens, where the roads were guarded by certain men ſo cruel, that no Chriſtian who paſſed that way could eſcape death, it pleaſed God that they were not ſlain, but captured, beaten, and bound, and were led before the Sultan. And being before him, Saint Francis, taught of the Holy Ghoſt, preached ſo divinely concerning the faith of Chriſt, how that for that faith he would even walk through fire. Upon which the Sultan began to feel exceeding great admiration for him, both for the Steadfaſtneſs of his Faith, and for the Contempt for the World which he perceived in him, — inaſmuch as he would receive no gift from him, being yet moſt poor, — and as well for the
martyr's

martyr's fervor, which was apparent in him. Thenceforth the Sultan hearkened unto him gladly, and begged him that he would return to him oft, freely conceding to him and to his Mates that they should preach wheresoever it seemed good to them; and he gave them a token, which should let no man offend them. . . . Finally, Saint Francis seeing by Divine Revelation that he could reap no more fruits in those parts, disposed all things to return with his Companions to the land of the Faithful; and calling them all together, he went into the presence of the Sultan, and took leave of him. And then said the Sultan unto him: "Brother Francis, I would gladly become a convert to the faith of Christ, but I fear to do so now; forasmuch, as should my people be ware of it, they would slay both you and me and all your Companions; and seeing that you may yet do many good works, and I have many weighty matters to despatch, I would not now occasion your death and mine. But teach me, I pray, how I may be saved; I am prepared to do that which you may lay upon me." Then said Saint Francis: "Sir, I now take my leave of you; but when that I am once more in mine own

own country and afcend into Heaven by the Grace of God; after my death, if it be pleafing in the fight of God, I will fend unto you two of my Brethren, from whom you fhall receive the holy baptifm of Chrift, and you fhall be faved, even as my Lord Jefus Chrift hath revealed unto me. And do you betwixt now and then defpatch all your matters, to the end that when the Grace of God fhall come to you it may find you well armed with faith and devotion." And thus he promifed to do and did. This done, Saint Francis returned home with the venerable train of his holy Companions, and after fome years Saint Francis by his bodily death rendered up his foul to God. And the Sultan falling ill was mindful of the promife of Saint Francis, and ftationed guards at certain points, and commanded that if two friars fhould appear clad in the garb of Saint Francis they fhould inftantly be brought before him. At that time Saint Francis appeared unto two friars, and charged them that they fhould go without delay unto the Sultan and procure his falvation, even as he had promifed: the which friars ftraightway arofe, and paffing over the fea, were by the faid said guards led before the Sultan; and seeing them, the Sultan rejoiced greatly and said: "Now, indeed, I know that God hath sent his servants unto me for my salvation, according to the promise made me by Saint Francis through divine Revelation." Receiving then the doctrines of the faith of Christ, and Holy Baptism of those same friars, thus born again in Christ, he died of that illness, and his soul was saved by the merits and the prayers of Saint Francis.

CHAPTER XXV.

How Saint Francis miraculously healed the Leper in Body and in Soul; and that which the Soul spake, ascending into Heaven.

THAT true disciple of Christ, Saint Francis, living in this miserable life, with all his strength strove ever to follow Christ, the Perfect Way, whence it ofttimes befell by divine action that whereas he healed a man's body, God did heal his soul in that selfsame hour, even as we read of Christ. And inasmuch as He not only freely became the servant of Lepers, but furthermore

more ordered that the Brothers of his Order, whether journeying or sojourning anywhere in this world, should become the servants of Lepers for the love of Christ, who for our love was fain to be held a Leper, it fell out that on a time at a Convent near which Saint Francis was then abiding, the Brethren were serving in a hospital for Lepers and infirm; in which was a Leper so peevish, so intolerable, and so arrogant that all men assuredly deemed, and so indeed it was, that he was possessed of a Devil, forasmuch as alike with words and with blows he terribly reviled all them that served him; nay, yet worse, he scandalously blasphemed against the blessed Christ and his most Holy Mother the Virgin Mary, so that none could in any wise be found who could or would serve him. And albeit the Brethren truly study meekly to endure injuries and insults to themselves, to the end that patience may have her perfect work, nevertheless, those to Christ and his Mother their consciences could not suffer, and every man among them determined to leave the said Leper: but this they would not do before they had duly declared their purpose unto Saint Francis, who was then abiding

abiding at a Convent hard by. And having ſignified to him their purpoſe, Saint Francis came unto that perverſe Leper; and drawing nigh to him, he greeted him, ſaying: "God grant thee peace, my beloved Brother." The Leper made anſwer, "What peace can I have of God, Which hath robbed me of peace and of every good thing, and hath made me all corrupt and ſtinking?" And Saint Francis ſaid, "Son, have patience, foraſmuch as the infirmities of the body are given us of God in this world for the ſalvation of our ſoul, they being of exceeding merit when they are borne meekly." The ſick man replied, "And can I endure the continual Pain that torments me night and day? And not only am I afflicted by mine infirmity, but far worſe do I ſuffer from the Brethren whom you have given me to wait upon me, and they ſerve me not as they ſhould." Then Saint Francis, knowing by a revelation that this Leper was poſſeſſed of an evil ſpirit, went out and prayed, and entreated God piouſly for him. And his prayer ended, he returned to him again and ſpake theſe words: "My Son, I myſelf will ſerve you, ſince you are ill-content with the others." "It pleaſeth me well,"

well," faid the fick man; "but what can you do for me more than the others?" Saint Francis anfwered, "Whatfoever you would that I fhould do." Said the Leper, "I would that you wafh me, every inch of me; forafmuch as fo terribly I ftink that I myfelf can ill endure it." Then Saint Francis ftraight commanded water to be heated with many fweet-fmelling herbs; then ftripping him, he began to wafh him with his own hands, another Brother pouring on the water; and by a divine miracle, wherefoever Saint Francis laid his holy hands upon him the Leprofy left him and his flefh remained perfectly found. And even as his flefh began to heal, fo too his foul began to be made whole; hence the Leper feeing himfelf beginning to be cured, began to have great compunction and repentance for his fins, and began to weep very bitterly; for as his body was cleanfed of the Leprofy from without by the wafhing of the water, even fo his foul was cleanfed of Sin from within by correction and tears. And being wholly healed, alike in body and in foul, he humbly confeffed himfelf guilty, and cried aloud, weeping: "Woe unto me, for I am worthy of Hell-fire

Hell-fire for the injuries and infults which I have heaped upon the Brethren, and for the peevifhnefs and blafphemy which I have manifefted towards God." Hence for two long weeks he perfevered in bitter tears for his fins, and in befeeching mercy from God, making ample confeffion to the Prieft. And Saint Francis, feeing fo plain a miracle, which God had wrought by his hand, gave thanks to the Lord and departed thence, going into remote countries: forafmuch as from Humility he defired to flee all Vainglory, and in all his acts fought only the Honor and Glory of God and not his own. Then, as was pleafing in the fight of God, the faid Leper, made whole in body and in foul, after two long weeks of penitence fell ill of another malady, and armed with the Sacraments of the Church he died a holy death, and his foul going into Paradife appeared in mid-air to Saint Francis, who was at prayer in a thick wood, and faid unto him, "Know you me?" "Who are you?" faid Saint Francis. "I am that Leper whom the bleffed Chrift healed for your merits, and to-day I enter into Eternal Life: for which I give thanks to God and to you. Bleffed be your foul and your body;

body; and bleſſed be your holy words and deeds; foraſmuch as through you many ſouls ſhall be ſaved in this world: and know that no day paſſeth in this world upon which the Holy Angels and the other Saints do not thank the Lord for the ſacred fruits which you and your Order have gathered in divers parts of the earth; and therefore be you greatly comforted and praiſe the Lord, and His bleſſing ſhall reſt upon your head." And ſaying theſe words he roſe into Heaven, and Saint Francis was left much comforted.

CHAPTER XXVI.

How Saint Francis converted three Thieves and Murderers, and made them Brethren; and of the moſt glorious Viſion beheld of one of them who was a moſt holy Brother.

SAINT FRANCIS went once through the deſert of Borgo to San Sepolcro, and paſſing by a Caſtle, which was called Monte Caſale, there came forth to meet him a noble and delicate Youth, who ſaid to him, "Father, I would gladly become one

one of your Brethren." Saint Francis anſwered him, "Son, you are young, delicate, and noble; peradventure you could not endure the poverty and rudeneſs of our life." And he ſaid, "Father, are ye not men like unto me? Then that which ye do bear can I alſo endure by the favor of Jeſus Chriſt." This anſwer was moſt pleaſing to Saint Francis; wherefore, bleſſing him, he ſtraightway received him into the Order and put upon him the name of Brother Angelo; and ſo worthily did the Youth comport himſelf, that but a brief ſpace thence Saint Francis made him Superior of that ſelfsame Convent of Monte Caſale. In thoſe days that region was infeſted by three thieves of much renown, who greatly plagued the land; the ſame came one day to the abode of the Brethren and prayed the ſaid Brother Angelo, the Superior, that he would feed them; and the Father Superior anſwered them after this faſhion, reproaching them ſorely: "You, Thieves and cruel Homicides, ye are not aſhamed to ſteal the wages of other men's toil; nay, more, bold and ſaucy that ye are, ye would fain devour the alms which are beſtowed upon the ſervants of God; ye are unworthy that the earth
ſhould

should sustain ye; forasmuch as ye have no reverence either for man, or for the God which created ye. Go, therefore, about your business, and appear no more within these walls;" upon which they, being disturbed, departed thence much wroth. And behold, Saint Francis returning home with bread and a small vessel of wine which he and his Companions had begged, and the Superior, narrating to him how he had driven those men thence, Saint Francis blamed him much, saying that he had borne himself barbarously; inasmuch as sinners were more readily led back to God by mildness than by fierce reproof: hence our Master Jesus Christ, whose Gospel we have promised to observe, said that He came not to heal those who were whole, but the sick; and that He came not to call the just but sinners to repent: wherefore many times He brake bread with them. Seeing, therefore, that you have sinned against charity and against the holy Gospel of Christ, I charge you by your vows of obedience that straightway you do take this Scrip with Bread, and this Vessel of Wine, and hasten after them, over mountains and through valleys, until you shall find them, and present them with this

this Bread and Wine in my name; and then fhall you kneel before them and humbly confefs to them your fin and your cruel conduct, and entreat them then in my name to do no more evil, but to fear God and offend no more againft His Holy Name; and if they will do fo, I promife to provide for their wants and to give them a conftant ftore to eat and to drink: and when that you have told them this, return hither humbly." While the faid Superior went forth to do Saint Francis' bidding, he fell on his knees and prayed God that He would foften the hearts of thofe Thieves and lead them to repent. The obedient Superior meeting them offered them the Bread and Wine and faid thofe words which Saint Francis had taught him. And as it pleafed God, thofe Thieves eating the alms beftowed by Saint Francis began to fay to one another: "Woe unto us, haplefs wretches! and what bitter pangs fhall we endure in Hell! For not only do we rob our fellow-men with ftripes and cruel blows, but we alfo flay them; nor for all thefe wicked and accurfed deeds which we do, do we feel any remorfe or fear of God, and behold this holy Brother, which hath followed us us hither for a few words with which he juſtly chid our Evil Craft, and hath humbly confeſſed to us his guilt, and moreover hath beſtowed on us Bread and Wine, and ſuch liberal promiſes from the Holy Father: verily theſe Holy Brethren are men of God, which are well worthy of Paradiſe; and we are ſons of everlaſting perdition, who are well worthy of the fires of Hell, and every day does but add to our perdition; and we know not whether for the many ſins which we have hitherto committed we can yet turn to the mercy of God." Theſe and ſimilar words being ſpoken by one among them, the others ſaid: "Surely you do ſpeak the truth, but what are we to do?" "Let us go," ſaid one, "to Saint Francis, and if he give us hope that we may ſtill appeal to the Mercy of God for our ſins, we will do whatſover he may command, and ſo we may ſet our ſouls free from the pains of Hell." This counſel was pleaſing in the ſight of the others; and all three agreeing together among themſelves proceeded in hot haſte to Saint Francis and ſaid to him thus: "Father, ſo great and ſo terrible are our ſins that we fear we can no longer turn to the Mercy of God: but if you have

have any hope that God will grant us His Mercy, behold we are ready to do whatfoever you fhall bid us, and to do penitence with you." Then Saint Francis, detaining them affectionately and with kindnefs, comforted them with many inftances, and affuring them of the Mercy of God, promifed them truly to entreat God for them, and fhowed them that the Mercy of God is infinite: and if we have an infinite number of fins, yet God's Mercy is greater ftill than our fins, according to the teachings of the Gofpel; and the Apoftle Paul faith, "Chrift came into the world to fave finners." Hearing thefe words, and other like teachings, the faid three Thieves renounced the Devil and all his works, Saint Francis received them into the Order, and they began to do fore penitence; and two of them lived not long after their converfion, and went thence to Paradife. But the third furviving, and meditating on his fins, gave himfelf such penitence to do, that for fifteen years continually, befide the ordinary fafts, which he obferved in common with the other Brothers, three days in every week he fafted upon bread and water, and went even barefoot, and with but a fingle tunic

to

to his back, sleeping never after Matins. About that time Saint Francis passed away from this miserable life. This Man having then continued the above penitence for many years, behold one night, after Matins, there came to him such a temptation to sleep, that in no manner could he hold out against it and watch, as was his wont. Finally, unable longer to resist or to pray, he went to his bed to slumber; and no sooner had he laid his head upon the pillow, than he was rapt in Ecstasy and led in spirit to a very high mountain, whereon was a most steep Precipice, and here and there were rocks shivered and splintered and rugged crags amid the rocks: at the sight of this cliff the Soul stood aghast. And the Angel who led this Brother seized him and cast him over the rugged edge of those rocks: and he, striking and rebounding from crag to crag and from stone to stone, at last attained the bottom of that precipice, as it seemed, all dismembered and torn; and lying thus in evil trim upon the ground, he who led him, said unto him, "Rise, for you have yet another journey to go." The Brother replied, "Meseems you be a most cruel and ill-advised ill-adviſed man, for ſeeing me thus dying of the fall which hath ſo ſhattered me, you yet bid me riſe." And the Angel approached him, and touching him, his every limb was made whole and he was healed perfectly. And then he ſhowed him a vaſt plain full of ſharp Stones and keen Thorns and Brambles; and he told him that he muſt needs run through all that plain and paſs barefoot unto the end, where he beheld a glowing Furnace, into which he muſt enter ſtraight. And the Brother having croſſed the plain with great anguiſh and pain, the Angel ſaid unto him, "Enter into that Furnace, for ſo it is ordered." The Friar replied, "Oh, woe is me! what a cruel guide have I! For you ſee me almoſt dead from that anguiſhing plain, and for all repoſe you bid me enter that glowing furnace." And gazing, he beheld many Demons around about the Furnace with iron pitchforks in their hands, with which, foraſmuch as he delayed to enter, they plunged him ſuddenly into the midſt of the fire. Having entered into the Furnace, gazing, he beheld a certain man which had been his Godfather, who burned apace with him; and he queſtioned him, ſaying, "O luckleſs Godfather, how came

came you hither?" And he anfwered, "Go but a little farther in and you fhall find my wife your Godmother, who will tell you the reafon of our damnation. The Brother going on, lo! there appeared to him the aforefaid Godmother all fmothered and fhut within a meafure of wheat blazing brightly; and he afked her, "O lucklefs and miferable Godmother, how have you come to fuch cruel torment?" And fhe anfwered, "Forafmuch as in the time of the great Famine, the which Saint Francis foretold, my hufband and I fold falfe meafure of wheat and of barley, and therefore do I burn bound within this meafure." And thefe words fpoken, the Angel which led the Friar haled him out of the Furnace, and then faid to him, "Prepare to take a horrid journey, which is yet to make." And he, lamenting, faid, "O harfheft of guides, who haft no Compaffion! you fee how I am almoft all burned in that Furnace, and yet you would lead me on a dangerous and horrid journey." And then the Angel touched him and made him whole and ftrong. Forthwith he led him to a bridge, the which could not be croffed without great danger, inafmuch as it was very

narrow

narrow and ſtraight, and moſt ſlippery, and without railing at either ſide ; and beneath it flowed a dreadful river, full of Serpents and Dragons and Scorpions, and it ſent up a moſt exceeding great ſtench ; and the Angel ſaid to him, "Croſs this Bridge, and you muſt croſs it from end to end." The Friar replied, " And how ſhall I croſs over, that I may not fall into that perilous flood?" The Angel ſaid, "Follow me, and place your foot where you ſhall ſee me place mine, and ſo you ſhall come ſafely over." The Brother paſſed behind the Angel, as he had taught him, until they came to the midſt of the Bridge ; and being thus midway the Angel flew thence, and departing from him went up into an exceeding high mountain which ſtood ſome diſtance from the Bridge ; and the Brother gazed long at the ſpot whither the Angel had flown : but remaining without a guide, and looking down, he ſaw thoſe ſo dreadful animals ſtanding with their heads out of the water, and with their mouths open ready to devour him if he ſhould fall : and he was in ſuch a terror that he in no wiſe knew what he ſhould do or ſay, foraſmuch as he could neither turn back nor go on. Hence, ſeeing
how

how great was his Tribulation, and that he had no other refuge ſave only God, he bowed his head and claſped the Bridge in his arms, and with his whole heart and with tears did commit himſelf to the care of God, that of His moſt Holy Mercy He might deign to help him. And having prayed, it ſeemed as if he began to put forth wings: at which he with great rejoicing awaited their further growing, that he might fly thence from the Bridge whither the Angel had flown before. But after a certain ſpace, for the great deſire which he had to croſs that Bridge, he began to fly; and becauſe, forſooth, his wings were not grown ſo much, he dropped back upon that Bridge and his feathers fell from him: upon which, yet again he hugged the bridge, and as before committed himſelf to the care of God; and having prayed, again he felt his wings ſprout forth; but as before he did not wait until they had gained their perfect growth: wherefore, ſtriving to fly before the time was ripe, he fell once more upon the Bridge and his feathers dropped yet again. For the which thing, ſeeing that he fell becauſe of his undue haſte to fly, he began to reaſon with himſelf: "Aſſuredly, if my

my wings sprout for the third time, I will wait until they are great enough for me to fly without another fall." And musing thus, he saw his wings put forth for the third time: and waiting a goodly space, until they should be very great, it seemed to him as if in the first and the second and the third sprouting of his wings had passed away five hundred years or more. At last he rose for the third time, and winged his flight with all his force, and flew high up to that same spot whither the Angel had flown, and knocking at the door of the Palace wherein he was, the door-keeper asked him, "Who art thou, who art come hither?" He answered, "I am a Gray Friar." The door-keeper said, "Await my coming, for I go to summon Saint Francis, to see if he know thee or no." Going thence for Saint Francis, he who was left behind fell to considering the marvellous walls of that Palace; and lo, those walls were translucent, and of such clearness that he did plainly see the choirs of Saints within and all those things that they did. And standing thus lost in wonder at this sight, lo! Saint Francis came and Brother Bernard and Brother Guy; and after these so great a multitude
of

of faints which had followed in their foot-fteps upon earth that they feemed almoft numberlefs: and Saint Francis, drawing near, faid to the door-keeper, "Let him enter in, forafmuch as he is one of my Brethren." And no fooner was he entered in than he felt fuch Confolation and fuch Sweetnefs that he forgot all the Tribulations which he had undergone, as if they had never been. And after Saint Francis, leading him by the hand, fhowed him many wondrous things, and after faid to him: "Son, you muft return to the world, where you fhall tarry feven days' fpace, wherein you fhall prepare yourfelf diligently with great devotion; forafmuch as after thofe feven days I fhall come for you, and then fhall you live with me in this abode of the Bleffed." Saint Francis was clad in a marvellous cloak, adorned with glittering Stars; and his five Wounds[1] were like unto five moft beauteous Stars, of fuch fplendor that the whole Palace fhone with their rays; and Brother Bernard had upon his head a crown of moft fair ftars; and Brother Guy was decked in wondrous light; and he recognized many other holy Friars in their midft

[1] The Stigmata.

midſt which he had never ſeen on earth. Thus diſmiſſed by Saint Francis, he returned, albeit reluctantly, to the world. Awaking and returning to his ſenſes and reviving, the Brothers were ringing the bells for Primes: ſo that that Viſion had endured no longer than from Matins unto Primes, although to him it ſeemed as it had endured for many years. And relating all this Viſion to his Superior in its due order, within ſeven days he began to grow fevered; and the eighth day Saint Francis came to fetch him, even as he had promiſed, with a vaſt multitude of glorious Saints, and took his ſoul thence to the Kingdom of the Bleſſed, unto Eternal Life.

CHAPTER XXVII.

How Saint Francis converted two Scholars of Bologna and made Friars of them; and then rid one of them of a ſore Temptation which beſet him.

SAINT FRANCIS once coming to the city of Bologna, all the people of that town ran out to ſee him: and ſo great was the

the preſs, that folk had much ado to gain the Market-place ; and the Market-place being filled full with men and women and ſcholars, Saint Francis aroſe in their midſt, and ſtanding upright, did begin to preach thoſe things which were taught him of the Holy Ghoſt : and ſo wondrous well did he preach, that it ſeemed an Angel preached rather than a man ; and his celeſtial words ſeemed as they were ſharp arrows, which pierced the hearts of all them that heard him, for by that preaching a vaſt hoſt of men and of women were converted to true repentance ; among the which were two noble ſtudents from the Marches of Ancona ; and the one was called by the name of Pilgrim and the other Rinieri ; which two after that ſame Sermon, touched to the ſoul by divine inſpiration, came unto Saint Francis ſaying that they deſired to forſake the world and all its pomp and become one with his Brethren. Then Saint Francis, knowing through revelation that they were ſent by God and that they were deſtined to lead a holy life within the Order, and conſidering their much fervor, received them joyfully, ſaying : " You, Pilgrim, ſhall follow the path of humility while in the Order

Order, and you, Brother Rinieri, ſhall wait upon the Brethren." And ſo it was; foraſmuch as Brother Pilgrim would never become a Prieſt, but remained a Lay Brother, although he was moſt learned, and very wiſe in canon law. Through this his humility he attained to exceeding great perfection of virtue, ſo much ſo that Brother Bernard, the eldeſt ſon of Saint Francis, ſaid of him that he was one of the moſt perfect Friars in this World. And finally the ſaid Brother Pilgrim, full of virtue, paſſed on from this life to the Bleſſed Life, working many miracles both before his death and after. And the ſaid Brother Rinieri devoutly and faithfully waited upon the Friars, living in great sanctity and humility; and he became moſt familiar with Saint Francis, and Saint Francis revealed many ſecret things to him. Being then made Miniſter of the Province of the Marches of Ancona, he long ruled in the utmoſt peace and diſcretion. After a certain ſpace God permitted a ſore Temptation to aſſail his ſoul; at which he, vaſtly troubled and vexed, afflicted himſelf with Faſtings, with Diſcipline, with Tears and with Prayers, by day and by night, and ſtill could not drive thence

thence that Temptation; but ofttimes he was in extreme defpair, inafmuch as for this thing he held himfelf to be forfaken of God. Being thus defperate, as a laft remedy he refolved to go to Saint Francis, thinking thus: "If Saint Francis look gracioufly upon me and receive me familiarly, as is his wont, I fhall believe that God will yet have compaffion upon me; but if not, it fhall be for a fign that my God has forfaken me." He therefore arofe and went unto Saint Francis, who at that time abode in the Palace of the Bifhop of Affifi grievoufly ill; and God revealed to him the whole manner of the temptation and defpair of the faid Brother Rinieri, and his purpofe and his coming. And ftraightway Saint Francis called Brother Leo and Brother Maximus, and faid to them: "Go forth to meet my beloved fon Brother Rinieri, and embrace him in my name, and greet him, and fay to him that of all the Brethren throughout the world I love him moft fingularly." They fet forth and met by the way Brother Rinieri, and embracing him they told him all thofe things which Saint Francis had charged them to fay. Hence fo much comfort and delight did

did flow into his ſoul, that he was almoſt beſide himſelf: and thanking God with his whole heart, he went on until he came to the place where Saint Francis lay ill. And albeit Saint Francis was grievously ill, neverthelefs hearing Brother Rinieri's approach, he roſe and went out to meet him, and embracing him moſt ſweetly, ſaid: "Brother Rinieri, my beloved ſon, of all the Brethren throughout the world moſt ſingularly do I love thee." And ſaying theſe words he made the ſign of the moſt Holy Croſs upon his brow, and after kiſſed him there. And then he ſaid: "My beloved ſon, God the Lord hath permitted this Temptation for your great increaſe in merit: but if you deſire not this increaſe, it ſhall not be thine." Wonderful to relate! So ſoon as Saint Francis had uttered theſe words, inſtantly all Temptation departed from him, as if he never in his life had felt aught of the kind, and he was left greatly comforted.

CHAPTER XXVIII.

Of an Ecſtaſy which ſeized upon Brother Bernard and held him from Matins even until Nones, he being all that ſpace unconſcious of Aught.

THE great favor which our Lord ofttimes ſhowed to thoſe poor Evangeliſts who forſook the world for love of Chriſt is ſet forth in Brother Bernard of Quintavalle, who, after taking on the habit of Saint Francis, was very many times abſorbed in God, in the contemplation of celeſtial things. Among others, it happened upon a time that being in Church hearkening to the Maſs, and ſtanding with his whole mind bent on God, he became ſo abſorbed and rapt in the Lord, that at the Elevation of the Hoſt he was conſcious of naught, neither knelt, nor bared his head, as did the others; but without once winking, did ſtand ſteadfaſtly gazing from the hour of Matins until Nones, as if inſenſible: and after Nones, returning to himſelf, did go about the Convent crying in tones of awe and wonder: "O Brothers! O Brothers! O Brothers! There is no man

man in this land so great, or so noble, to whom, were he promised a most beauteous palace filled with gold, it were not easy to bear most loathsome burdens, to gain so rare a treasure." Now the mind of the aforesaid Brother Bernard was so bent upon this Celestial Treasure promised to all true lovers of God, that for fifteen years continually he went ever with his head and face upraised to heaven; and in all that time he satisfied never his hunger at table, albeit he ate of that which was put before him a little, forasmuch as he said that the mere fact of eating naught constitutes not perfect abstinence, but true abstinence is to be temperate in all things which are savory in the mouth; and thereby he attained to such clearness and light of intellect that even the great Doctors of the Church had recourse to him for the solution of knotty questions and hard passages of Scripture; and he made plain every puzzle to them, and inasmuch as his mind was freed and abstracted from all earthly things, he, after the manner of a Swallow, flew oft aloft in thought; hence sometimes twenty days and sometimes thirty days he would abide alone upon the top of very high

high mountains musing upon celestial matters. Wherefore Brother Guy spoke concerning him, saying that this gift was not given to other men which was given to Brother Bernard of Quintavalle; which is to say, that he fed upon the wing like the Swallow; and for this excellent grace, given him of God, Saint Francis gladly and often held converse with him both night and day. Hence they were at certain times found the whole night long absorbed in God in the thick wood, where they had met together to discourse of Him.

CHAPTER XXIX.

How the Devil ofttimes did appear in the Form of One Crucified unto Brother Rufus, telling him that all his Labor was vain, inasmuch as he was not chosen unto Eternal Life: Saint Francis learning this through Divine Revelation, showed Brother Rufus the Error in which he lay.

BROTHER RUFUS, one of the most noble men of the city of Assisi, and a comrade of Saint Francis, a man of exceeding

exceeding fanctity, was upon a time forely tempted and tormented in fpirit concerning the doctrine of Predeftination; wherefore he was moft melancholy and fad; inafmuch as the Devil put it into his heart that he was damned and was not one of thofe elected unto Eternal Life, and that all the good works which he wrought in the Order would avail him naught. And this temptation enduring day after day, he for fheer fhame forbearing to reveal aught of it to Saint Francis, yet paufed not in praying and fafting: for which thing the Enemy began to heap forrow upon forrow, befides the inner battle, fhaking him from without with evil vifions. Hence he once appeared to him in the form of One Crucified, faying unto him: "O Brother Rufus, why fhould you thus afflict yourfelf with penitence and prayers, forafmuch as you are not one of the Elect? And believe me, that I know them whom I have chofen and predeftined; and put not your faith in the fon of Peter Bernardone,[1] albeit he may tell you to the contrary, and moreover queftion him not concerning fuch matters, fince neither he nor any man elfe can know, fave only I, Who

[1] Saint Francis.

Who am the Son of God: wherefore of a verity you may believe me, that you are of the number of the damned; and the ſon of Peter Bernardone, your father,[1] and alſo his father, are damned, and whoſover ſhall follow after them is deceived and miſled." And hearing theſe words, Brother Rufus began to be ſo overſhadowed by the Prince of Darkneſs, that already he loſt all faith and love which he cheriſhed for Saint Francis, and cared not to tell him aught of theſe things. But that which Brother Rufus told not to the Holy Father was made known to him of the Holy Ghoſt; hence Saint Francis ſeeing in ſpirit the great danger of the ſaid Brother, ſent Brother Maximus to ſummon him; to whom Brother Rufus made anſwer ſcornfully, "What have I to do with Brother Francis?" And then Brother Maximus, filled full with divine wiſdom, knowing the deceitful wiles of the Devil, ſaid: "O Brother Rufus, know you not that Brother Francis is like to an Angel of God, which hath enlightened ſo many ſouls in this world, and from which we receive the Grace

---

[1] That is, the founder of the Order to which he belonged.

Grace of God? Wherefore I would that at all hazards you come before his face with me; forafmuch as I fee clearly that you are led aftray of the Devil." And having faid this, Brother Rufus was moved, and went forth to Saint Francis, and Saint Francis feeing him from afar began to cry aloud, "O wicked Brother Rufus, in whom have you trufted?" And Brother Rufus drawing near to him, he told him in due order all his temptation brought upon him by the Devil from within and from without, and clearly fhowed him that he who had appeared to him was the Devil and not Chrift, and that in no manner muft he confent to his fuggeftions; but when the Devil fhould again fay to him, "You are damned," he fhould make anfwer, "Open your mouth;" "and this fhall be for a fign unto you that he is the Devil and not Chrift: for fo foon as you have given him this anfwer, ftraightway he fhall flee thence. By another token alfo fhall you know that he is the Devil, forafmuch as he hath hardened your heart againft all goodnefs, which thing is proper to his office; but Chrift the Bleffed did never yet make hard the heart of the faithful, but rather foftens it, even

as

as is fpoken by the mouth of the Prophet: 'I will take the ftony heart out of their flefh, and will give them a heart of flefh.'" Then Brother Rufus, feeing that Saint Francis had related to him in due order all the manner of his temptation, ftung by his words, began to weep very fore and to adore Saint Francis, and humbly to acknowledge his fin, in that he had hidden his temptation. And thus he was left much comforted and confoled by the admonitions of the Holy Father, and quite changed for the better. Then finally Saint Francis faid to him: "Go, fon, and confefs your fin, nor give over your wonted prayers: and know of a certainty that this temptation fhall be of great ufe and comfort to you, and in a brief fpace you fhall fo prove it." Brother Rufus returned again to his cell in the foreft; and praying there with many tears, lo! the enemy came again in the femblance of Chrift, that is in his outward feeming, and faid to him: "O Brother Rufus, did I not tell you to put not your faith in the fon of Peter Bernardone, and that you fhould not weary yourfelf with tears and prayers, fince you are damned? What avails it to afflict yourfelf yourſelf while you live, and then when you die, ſtill you will be damned?" And ſuddenly Brother Rufus replied to the Devil, "Open thy mouth that I may ſpit upon thee." At which the Devil, waxing wrath, ſtraightway departed thence with ſuch a tempeſt of wind and ſo great a rain of ſtones from Mount Subaſſio, which was in that neighborhood, that the noiſe of the ſtones which fell down was heard for a great ſpace round about; and ſo great was the tumult that they made, together with the rumbling, that horrid flames of fire flaſhed through the valleys, and at the ſound that they made, Saint Francis with his Companions came out from the Convent in great amaze, to ſee what ſtrange thing this might be; and even unto this day men may ſee that exceeding great waſte of ſtones. Then Brother Rufus ſaw plainly that this was the Devil which had miſled him. And returning again to Saint Francis, again he fell before him on the ground and confeſſed his fault. Saint Francis comforted him with ſweet words, and ſent him again conſoled to his cell, wherein he, praying moſt devoutly, Chriſt the Bleſſed appeared to him, and fired all his ſoul with Divine

Divine Love and said, "Well doft thou, son, to put thy faith in Brother Francis, forafmuch as he who afflicted thee was the Devil; but I am Chrift thy Mafter: and that you may be well affured of this, I give you this sign: while you live, you fhall never know any forrow, neither any grief." And saying thefe words, Chrift departed thence, leaving him with fuch Rejoicing and fuch fweetnefs of fpirit and elevation of mind that day and night he was abforbed and rapt in God. And from that time forth he was fo confirmed in Grace and in the fure fenfe of his Salvation, that he was wholly changed to another man; and he would fain have remained day and night in prayer and in contemplation of Divine Things, would others have but let him. Hence Saint Francis faid concerning him, that Brother Rufus was canonized of Chrift in this life, and that fave in his prefence he hefitated not to call him Saint Rufus, albeit he yet lived upon this earth.

CHAPTER XXX.

Of the glorious Sermon which Saint Francis and Brother Rufus preached at Aſſiſi.

THE ſaid Brother Rufus, through continual contemplation, grew to be ſo abſorbed in God that he became almoſt dumb and inſenſible, and but very rarely ſpoke; and withal he had not the Grace, nor the Valor, nor the Eloquence to preach: and neverthelefs Saint Francis charged him upon a time that he ſhould go to Aſſiſi, and ſhould preach to the people even as the Lord ſhould inſpire him. To which Brother Rufus made anſwer: "Reverend Father, I beſeech you, pardon me and ſend me not forth, inaſmuch as you are well aware that I have no grace in preaching, and am ſimple and unlearned." And then ſaid Saint Francis: "Foraſmuch as you have not obeyed promptly, I command you by your ſacred vow of Obedience that you go, clad only in your breeches, unto Aſſiſi, and enter there a church and preach to the people." Upon this command the ſaid Brother Rufus laid off his raiment and went

went to Affifi and entered into a church, and doing reverence to the altar, went up into the pulpit and began to preach; at which thing the men and boys began to laugh, and faid, "Lo, one who doth penitence, left he grow proud and vain." Meantime Saint Francis, pondering on the ready obedience of Brother Rufus, which was one of the nobleft gentlemen of Affifi, and of the hard command which he had laid upon him, began to reproach himfelf, faying, "Whence haft thou fuch prefumption, fon of Peter Bernardone, thou vile and petty fellow, that thou fhouldft command Brother Rufus, which is one of the nobleft gentlemen of Affifi, to go forth and preach to the people even as he were mad? In God's name, go forth thou likewife, and prove for thyfelf even that thou haft commanded of others." And fuddenly, in the ardor of his fpirit, he alfo laid off his raiment and went forth to Affifi, and with him went Brother Leo bearing his habit and that of Brother Rufus. And the men of Affifi feeing them in like plight, fcoffed at them, holding that they with Brother Rufus were made mad by much Penitence. Saint Francis entered into the church

church where Brother Rufus was preaching thefe words: "Fly, my beloved, from the World, and forfake Sin; covet not the goods of others, if you would efcape Hell; follow God's commands, love God and your neighbor, if you would gain Heaven; do penitence, if you would poffefs the Kingdom of Heaven." Then Saint Francis went up into the pulpit; and he began to preach fo marvelloufly of the Vanity of the world, of holy Penitence, of voluntary Poverty, and of the longing after the Celeftial Kingdom, and of the nakednefs and fcorn of the Paffion of our Lord Jefus Chrift, that all they who heard his preaching, men and women in great multitudes, began to weep violently with admirable devotion and contrition; and not only here, but throughout all Affifi, upon that day fuch floods of tears were fhed for Chrift's Paffion, that nothing fimilar was ever feen. And the people being thus edified and confoled by the act of Saint Francis and Brother Rufus, Saint Francis clad again both Brother Rufus and himfelf; and thus reclad they returned back to the Convent of Portiuncula, praifing and glorifying God, Who had given them grace to win the victory over felf by their felf-contempt,

contempt, and to edify the flock of Chriſt Jeſus by their good Example, and to ſhow what it is to deſpiſe the World; and that day ſo great was the devotion which the people felt for them, that he held himſelf bleſſed who could but touch the hem of their garments.

CHAPTER XXXI.

How Saint Francis duly knew the ſecret Souls of all his Brethren.

EVEN as our Lord Jeſus Chriſt ſaith in the Gospel, "I know my ſheep and they know me," etc., ſo the bleſſed Father Saint Francis, like unto a good ſhepherd, knew all the merits and virtues of his Companions by divine revelations, and even ſo was made aware of their defects; for the which thing he knew how to provide for each the beſt remedy, which is to ſay, he humbled the Proud, exalted the Lowly, inveighed againſt Vice, and lauded Virtue, according as may be read in the wondrous revelations which he had concerning his firſt family. Among the ſame we learn that Saint

Saint Francis once being with the said family in a certain place discoursing of God, Brother Rufus was not among them to hearken unto this discourse, but was lost in a muse in the midst of the wood; proceeding with their discourse of God, lo! Brother Rufus came forth from the wood and passed by somewhat remote from them. Then Saint Francis, seeing him, turned again to his Companions and asked them, saying: "Tell me, whose think you is the holiest soul which God hath sent into the world?" And they made answer, saying that they believed it to be his own. And Saint Francis said to them: "Beloved Brethren, I know myself to be the most unworthy and the vilest man whom God hath sent into this world; but see ye not that same Brother Rufus, who even now came forth from the wood? God hath revealed to me that his soul is one of the three most holy souls in the world: and verily I say unto you that I should not hesitate to call him Saint Rufus while he yet lives, forasmuch as his soul is confirmed in grace and sanctified and canonized in Heaven of our Lord Jesus Christ." And these words Saint Francis uttered not before

fore the face of the said Brother Rufus. How Saint Francis likewise knew the faults of his Brethren may be clearly seen in Brother Elias, whom ofttimes he reproved for his pride; and in Brother John of the Choir, to whom he did prophesy that he should go out and hang himself by the neck; and in that Friar whom the Devil held fast by the throat when he was corrected for his disobedience; and in many other Friars, whose secret faults and virtues he knew clearly through a revelation from Christ.

XXXII.

How Brother Maximus entreated of Christ the Virtue of Meekness.

THE first Companions of Saint Francis strove with all their strength to be poor in worldly goods and rich in virtues, by which they might gain true riches, celestial and eternal. It happened one day, that they being met together to talk of God, one of them related this parable: "There was a certain man who was a dear friend of God, and had great gifts alike for

a life of action and of contemplation, and withal had such exceeding meekness, that he held himself as the greatest of sinners: which meekness sanctified and strengthened him in grace, and made him grow continually in virtue and in the favor of God, and never let him fall into any manner of sin." Brother Maximus hearing such marvellous things concerning meekness, and knowing that it was a treasure of eternal life, began to be so inflamed with love and longing for this virtue of meekness, that, raising his eyes with great fervor to Heaven, he made a vow and most certain promise never more to be merry in this world until he should feel the said virtue abiding perfectly within him; and from that time forth he would pass almost the entire day shut up within his cell, mortifying himself with fasts, vigils, prayers, and extreme lamentations and tears before God, to the end that he might wring from Him this virtue, wanting which he held himself worthy of Hell, and with which that friend of God, as he had heard, was so plentifully endowed. And Brother Maximus, cherishing thus this desire for many days, it came to pass that he one day entered into a wood, and in the fervor of his
spirit

ſpirit wandered on, weeping, ſighing, groaning, and beſeeching with ardent longing that God would grant him that divine virtue: and foraſmuch as the Lord gladly hears the prayers of the contrite and the lowly, Brother Maximus being thus forlorn, a Voice came down from Heaven, and the ſame called him twice: "Brother Maximus, Brother Maximus!" And he, having ſpiritual knowledge that this was the Voice of Chriſt, replied: "My Lord!" And Chriſt ſaid to him: "What will you give to have this Grace that you aſk?" Brother Maximus replied: "Lord, I will give the eyes out of my head." And Chriſt ſaid to him: "And I deſire that you have the Grace, and likewiſe the eyes." And ſaying this, the Voice vaniſhed; and Brother Maximus was left behind filled with ſo much grace of the deſired virtue of meekneſs and of the Light of God, that from that time forth he went ever rejoicing; and ofttimes when he prayed, did rejoice aloud, making a dull noiſe like that of a dove, — *oo, oo, oo,* — and with a ſhining countenance and a light heart he would linger thus loſt in contemplation; and withal, being become very meek, he held himſelf to be leſs than all other men.

Being

Being aſked by Brother James, of Fallerone, why in his rejoicing he changed not ever his tune, he replied with great cheer, That when one thing containeth all good, it boots not to change the meaſure or the tune.

CHAPTER XXXIII.

How Saint Clara, at the Command of the Pope, bleſſed the Bread which was on the Table: whereat on every Loaf was ſeen the ſign of the Holy Croſs.

SAINT CLARA, that moſt devout follower of the Croſs of Chriſt, and the noble offspring of Saint Francis, was of ſuch ſanctity that not alone Biſhops and Cardinals but even the Pope himſelf longed with great affection to ſee and to hear her, and many times viſited her in perſon. Among other times, the Holy Father once went to Moniſtero to hear her converſe of celeſtial and divine things; and being thus met together, reaſoning of divers matters, Saint Clara meantime bade them make ready the tables, and place upon them bread,

bread, to the end that the Holy Father might blefs it; whence, her fpiritual difcourfe completed, Saint Clara, kneeling with exceeding great reverence, prayed him that it might pleafe him to blefs the bread upon the table. The Holy Father replied: "Sifter Clara, moft faithful among women, I defire that you do blefs thefe loaves, making above them the fign of Chrift's Holy Crofs, to which you have given yourfelf entirely, body and foul." Saint Clara faid: "Pardon me, Moft Holy Father, for I fhould be worthy of great reproach if before the face of Chrift's Vicar on earth, I, who am but a vile and filly woman, fhould venture to give fuch bleffing." And the Pope made anfwer: "To the end that it be not reputed prefumption, but merely righteous fubmiffion, I charge you, by your facred vow of Obedience, to make the fign of the moft Holy Crofs above thefe loaves, bleffing them in the name of God." Then Saint Clara, like a true daughter of Obedience, did devoutly blefs the bread with the fign of the moft Holy Crofs. Wonderful to relate! Suddenly upon all thofe loaves appeared the fign of the Crofs moft beauteoufly carven.
Then

Then of thofe loaves a part were eaten, and a part preferved in token of the miracle. And the Holy Father, after that he had feen that miracle, partaking of the faid bread and giving thanks to God, departed thence, leaving Saint Clara with his bleffing. In thofe days Sifter Ortolana, the mother of Saint Clara, abode in the Convent, and Sifter Agnes, her fifter, both of them together with Saint Clara, full of virtue and of the Holy Ghoft, and with many other Nuns; unto whom Saint Francis fent many that were fick and infirm; and they by their prayers and by the fign of the moft Holy Crofs healed them all every one.

CHAPTER XXXIV.

How Saint Louis, King of France, went in Perfon, in the Guife of a Pilgrim, to Perugia, to vifit Holy Brother Guy.

SAINT LOUIS, King of France, once went on a pilgrimage to fee the holy places of the world: and hearing the exceeding great fame of the fanctity of Brother Guy, who was one of the firft followers of Saint

Saint Francis, he felt a hearty defire, and at length determined to vifit him in perfon; for the which purpofe he came to Perugia, where the faid Brother Guy was then abiding. And drawing nigh to the gate of the Monaftery, in the guife of a poor and unknown pilgrim, with but a few Companions, he moft perfiftently demanded Brother Guy, faying to the gate-keeper naught of who he was that afked for him. The gate-keeper then went to Brother Guy and told him that a pilgrim ftood without the gate and afked for him: and God revealed and made known to him that this was the King of France: at which fuddenly he with great fervor left his cell and ran forth to the gate; and without further queftioning, and before even they had fet eyes each upon the other, kneeling with extreme devotion, they embraced and kiffed with much familiarity, as they had long been bound by the bonds of friendfhip: but withal they fpoke no word, neither the one nor the other; but ftood thus embraced in filence with thefe tokens of affectionate amity. And having remained thus for a fpace without fpeaking a word together, they parted one from the other;
and

and Saint Louis departed thence on his journey, and Brother Guy returned again to his cell. The King being departed, a Friar asked a certain one among his Brethren who that man might be who had so ardently embraced Brother Guy; and he made answer that it was Louis, King of France, who had come thither to see Brother Guy. The same being repeated to the other Monks, they were sore afflicted that Brother Guy had spoken no word with him; and reproving him, they said: "O Brother Guy, wherefore were you so churlish, as when so holy a King came hither from France to see you and to hear wise words from your lips, you spake not unto him?" Brother Guy made answer: "My beloved Brothers, marvel not hereat: forasmuch as neither I could speak a word to him nor he to me; inasmuch as so soon as we were embraced, the light of Divine Wisdom revealed and laid bare his heart to me and mine to him; and thus by Divine Authority gazing each into the other's heart, we knew far better those things which he might have spoken to me and I to him, than had we spoken them with our lips, and with greater comfort than had we striven to set forth

forth with our voices thofe things which we felt in our hearts; whereas the human tongue being but faulty and ill-fitted to exprefs clearly the fecret myfteries of God, it would have rather added to our difcomfiture than our confolation; wherefore know that the King departed hence from me wondrous well content and comforted in fpirit."

CHAPTER XXXV.

How, being infirm, Saint Clara was borne by a Miracle unto the Church of St. Francis, upon Chriftmas Night, and heard Mafs therein.

SAINT CLARA being once infirm of body, fo that fhe could in no manner go forth to fay Mafs in Church with the other Nuns, when the folemn feaft of the Nativity of Chrift was at hand all the others went to Matins; and fhe remained behind in bed ill content that fhe could not go forth with the reft to receive that fpiritual comfort. But Jefus Chrift, her heavenly Spoufe, loath to leave her fo ill content, had her borne by miraculous power unto the Church of St. Francis, and thus was fhe prefent at the

the office of Matins and at the Midnight Mafs; moreover, did receive Holy Communion, and was then tranfported again to her bed. The Nuns returning back to Saint Clara, fervice being ended at St. Damian's, faid to her: "Oh, our Mother, Sifter Clara, what exceeding confolation has been ours at this facred feaft of the Nativity! Would it had pleafed God that you might have been among us!" And Saint Clara replied: "Thankfgiving and praife give I unto Our Lord Chrift Jefus; may His name be bleffed, my beloved Sifters and Daughters, forafmuch as I have witneffed every folemn rite of this moft holy night, and even greater things than you have feen, to the great confolation of my foul: forafmuch as through the interceffion of my Father Saint Francis, and by the Grace of our Lord Jefus Chrift, I was prefent in the Church of my venerable Father Saint Francis, and heard all the Office with my bodily as well as my fpiritual ears, and the found of the organ as it was played; and there too I did partake of the moft Holy Communion. Wherefore for all thefe mercies vouchfafed to me, rejoice greatly and thank our Lord Jefus Chrift.

CHAPTER XXXVI.

How Saint Francis set forth to Brother Leo a fair Vision which he saw.

UPON a time Saint Francis was sore infirm, and Brother Leo served him; the said Brother Leo, being at prayer beside Saint Francis, was rapt in Ecstasy, and borne in spirit to an exceeding great stream, broad and brawling. And standing there to note who should pass over, he saw certain heavily-laden Friars enter the Flood, the which were straightway beaten down by the rushing waters and were drowned; certain others came a third of the way over; others reached the middle of the Flood; certain others came almost over to the other shore; who all, from the violence of the Flood, and from the burdens which they bare upon their backs, fell at last and perished miserably. Seeing this, Brother Leo was much moved to pity: and suddenly standing thus, behold there came a great multitude of Monks, without burden or weight or any other thing, whose countenances shone with the light of Holy Poverty;

erty; and they entered upon the waters, and paſſed over without any danger; and ſeeing this, Brother Leo returned to himſelf. And then Saint Francis, feeling in ſpirit that Brother Leo had ſeen ſome Viſion, called him unto his bedſide and aſked him concerning thoſe things which he had ſeen. And Brother Leo relating duly all his Viſion, Saint Francis ſaid: "That which you have ſeen is true. The great river is this world; the Brethren which were drowned in the Flood are they who forſake the calling of the Evangeliſts, and above all elſe attain not unto the moſt extreme poverty; but they who paſſed over unharmed are thoſe Monks who ſeek after naught earthly or carnal, neither poſſeſs aught of this world's goods, but having naught ſave a modicum of food and raiment, therewith are well content, following Chriſt naked on the Croſs; and they do bear cheerfully and willingly the burden and the ſweet yoke of Chriſt and of their ſacred vow of Obedience; and hence they paſs eaſily from temporal unto Eternal Life.

CHAPTER XXXVII.

How Jesus Christ the Blessed, at the Request of Saint Francis, did convert a rich and noble Knight, and make him a Monk, the Same having made great Proffers and paid much Honor unto Saint Francis.

SAINT FRANCIS, the servant of Christ, coming late one night unto the house of a great and powerful lord, was received and entertained of him, he and his Companion, even as they had been Angels of God, with exceeding courtesy and devotion: for the which thing Saint Francis held him in much esteem, considering that upon his entering into the house he had embraced and kissed him with extreme amity, and thereafter had washed his feet and dried them and kissed them humbly, and had made a great fire, and laying the table with many rich meats, continually did serve on him with shining face while he ate thereof. Now Saint Francis having eaten, together with his Companion, this gentleman said: "Lo, my Father, I and all my worldly goods are thine: whensoever
ever

ever thou doſt want raiment or mantle or whatſoever thing, buy, and I will pay the price; and behold, I am ready to provide for thine every want, foraſmuch as by the Grace of God I have wherewithal ſo to do, inaſmuch as I abound in all temporal goods; and hence for love of God Who gave them, I cheerfully do good unto His poor." Upon which Saint Francis, ſeeing him poſſeſſed of ſuch courteſy and blandneſs, and the bounty which he proffered, conceived ſuch affection for him that, departing thence, he ſaid to his Comrade as he went: "Verily this gentleman would well beſeem our Religion and Company, being ſo grateful and ſo pleaſing unto God, and ſo loving and courteous towards his fellow-men and to the poor. Know, beloved Brother, that Courteſy is one of the eſſential qualities of God, Who maketh His ſun to ſhine and His rain to fall upon the juſt and upon the unjuſt, through Courteſy: and Courteſy is alſo the ſiſter of Charity, which puts out Hatred and preſerves Love alive. Becauſe I have known ſo much divine virtue in this good man, I would gladly take him for my Companion: and hence I deſire that we may one day return again

again unto him, if haply God may touch his heart and move him to go along with us to enter upon the ſervice of God; and meantime we will pray God that He may breathe this deſire into his heart, and give him grace to execute it." Wonderful to relate! A few days thence, Saint Francis having prayed, our Lord breathed this deſire into the heart of that gentleman. And Saint Francis ſpake to his Companion, ſaying: "Let us go forth, my Brother, to the abode of that courteous man; foraſmuch as I have firm faith in God, that he in the Courteſy of temporal things ſhall give himſelf to us and become our Companion." And they went forth; and drawing nigh to his houſe, Saint Francis ſpake to his Companion, ſaying: "Await me here a little, foraſmuch as I am fain firſt to pray to God that it may pleaſe Him to proſper our journey; that it may pleaſe Chriſt Jeſus to grant unto us poor weak men the noble prey which we hope to capture from the world through the virtue of His moſt Holy Paſſion." And ſaying this, he began to pray at a place whence he might be ſeen of the ſaid courteous man; hence, as it pleaſed God, that ſame, gazing hither and yon,
ſoon

soon saw Saint Francis lost in most devout prayer before Christ, Who with great splendor appeared to him in the said prayer and stood before his face; and as he abode there thus, he saw Saint Francis for a good space lifted up bodily from the earth. For the which thing he was so moved of God and inspired to forsake the world, that presently he went forth from his palace, and in the fervor of his spirit hastened towards Saint Francis; and drawing nigh unto him as he prayed, he knelt before his feet, and with exceeding great urgency and devotion he besought that it might please him to receive him and to let him do penitence with him. Then Saint Francis, seeing that his prayers had been heard of God, and that the selfsame thing which he desired, this gentleman besought with such urgency, he raised him up, and fervently and joyously embraced and kissed him, most devoutly thanking God, Which had added so noble a knight to his Company. And that gentleman said to Saint Francis: "What commandest thou me to do, my Father? Lo, I am ready for thy command, and to give to the poor all that that I have, and to follow after Christ with thee, thus set free of all temporal

temporal burden." And even so he did, according unto the counsel of Saint Francis; for he shared his goods among the poor, and entered into the Order, and lived in great penitence and sanctity of life, and in honest conversation with his Brethren.

CHAPTER XXXVIII.

How Saint Francis had spiritual Knowledge that Brother Elias was damned, and was destined to die outside of the Order; wherefore at Brother Elias' Entreaty He prayed to God in his Behalf and was heard.

SAINT FRANCIS and Brother Elias once abiding together in the selfsame Convent, Saint Francis had a revelation from God that Brother Elias was damned, and was destined to renounce his faith and finally to die outside of the Order. For the which thing Saint Francis conceived such displeasure against him, that for a space he spake not to him, neither held he any converse with him; and if at any time it happened that Brother Elias came forth to meet him, he would turn aside and take another

another road, that he might not meet with him; at which Brother Elias began to note and to underſtand that Saint Francis was much diſpleaſed with him; hence, deſiring to know the cauſe, he one day accoſted Saint Francis to ſpeak with him; and Saint Francis ſhunning Brother Elias, he retained him courteouſly perforce, and began to entreat him diſcreetly that it would pleaſe him to ſignify to him the cauſe for which he thus ſhunned his company and all converſe with him. And Saint Francis made anſwer: "The cauſe is namely this: foraſmuch as it has been revealed to me of God that you for your ſins ſhall renounce your faith and ſhall die outſide of the Order, and alſo God hath revealed to me that you are accurſed and damned." Hearing this, Brother Elias ſpake thus: "Reverend Father, I beſeech you for the love of Jeſus Chriſt that you ſhun me not for this, neither drive me from you; but like unto a good Shepherd, following after the example of Chriſt, recover and receive again the ſheep which muſt periſh if you aid him not; and pray unto God for me that, if it may be, He revoke the ſentence of my damnation; foraſmuch as it is written that God will
change

change His decree if the finner turn from his fin: and fo great is my faith in your prayers, that were I in the midmoft part of Hell and you fent up a prayer to God for me, I fhould feel a certain eafe; therefore I pray you yet again to recommend me, a finner, unto God, Which came into the world to fave finners, that He will grant me His Mercy." And this Brother Elias faid with great devotion, ay, even with tears; upon which Saint Francis, like a pious Father, promifed to pray to God for him; and fo he did. And praying to God very fervently for him, he knew by revelation that his prayer was heard of God, in fo far as concerned the revocation of the fentence of Brother Elias' damnation, for finally his foul fhould not be damned; but affuredly he would forfake the Faith and die outfide the Order. And even fo it happened; forafmuch as Frederic, King of Sicily, rebelling againft the Church, and being excommunicated by the Pope, he and whofoever fhould give him aid or counfel, the faid Brother Elias, who was held to be one of the moft wife men in the world, being fummoned by that fame King Frederic, joined himfelf unto him, and became a rebel to the Church and an apoftate

tate from the Order: for the which thing he was excommunicated of the Pope, and ſtripped of his habit by Saint Francis. And being thus excommunicate, and falling very ill, a certain lay Brother among his Brethren, which had remained in the Order and was a man of good and honeſt life, hearing of his fore infirmity, went to viſit him; and among other matter ſaid to him: "My beloved Brother, it grieves me much that you ſhould be excommunicate and driven out from your Order, and that even ſo you muſt die; but if you can perceive any mode or manner by which I may refcue you out of your peril, I will cheerfully endure any ſuffering for your ſake." Brother Elias made anſwer: "My Brother, I ſee no other manner than that you ſhould betake yourſelf to the Pope, and entreat him that for the love of God, and of Saint Francis his ſervant, through whoſe admonitions I was led to forſake the world, he abſolve me from his excommunication and reſtore to me the habit of my Order." Thus he ſpake to his Brother, who cheerfully undertook any labor ſo that he might but be ſaved: and departing thence from him, he threw himſelf at the feet of the Holy

Holy Father, humbly befeeching him that he would fhow mercy to his Brother, for love of Chrift and of Saint Francis his fervant. And as it pleafed God, the Pope granted him his leave to return again, and if he found Brother Elias ftill alive, abfolve him in his name from excommunication, and reftore to him his habit; upon which he fet forth rejoicing, and with great fpeed came again to Brother Elias, and found him alive, albeit at the point of death, and fet him free from the ban of the Church; and putting on him again his habit, Brother Elias paffed away from this life, and his foul was faved through the merits of Saint Francis and by his prayers, in which Brother Elias had put fuch great faith.

CHAPTER XXXIX.

Of the Marvellous Sermon which was preached in the Confiftory by Saint Antony of Padua, a Gray Friar.

THAT marvellous veffel of the Holy Ghoft, Saint Antony of Padua, one of the chofen Difciples and Companions of of Saint Francis, who was called of Saint Francis his Vicar, once preached in the Confiftory before the Pope and his Cardinals; in which Confiftory there were men of divers nations; namely, Greeks, Latins, French, Germans, Slavs, and Englifh, and men fpeaking other divers tongues. Fired by the Holy Ghoft, fo efficacioufly, fo devoutly, fo fubtly, fo fweetly, fo clearly, and fo plainly did he fet forth the Word of God, that all they which were prefent at the Confiftory, of whatfoever divers tongues they were, clearly underftood all his words diftinctly, even as he had fpoken in the language of each man among them; and they all were ftruck dumb with amaze, and it feemed as that ancient miracle of the Apoftles had been renewed, when as at the time of the Pentecoft they fpake by virtue of the Holy Ghoft in every tongue; and they faid one to another with admiration and awe: "Is not he who preaches come out from Spain? and how do we hear in his difcourfe every man of us the fpeech of his own land?" Likewife the Pope, confidering and marvelling at the profundity of his words, faid: "Verily this man is the Ark of the Covenant and the Vehicle of the Holy Gofpel."

CHAPTER XL.

Of the Miracle which God performed when Saint Antony, being at Rimini, preached to the Fiſhes of the Sea.

OUR Bleſſed Lord and Saviour Jeſus Chriſt, deſiring to ſet forth the great ſanctity of His moſt faithful ſervant Saint Antony, how devout a thing it was to hear his preaching and his Holy Doctrines, He reproved the folly of heretics and infidels through unreaſoning beaſts, notably the fiſhes, as of old in the Bible He chid the ignorance of Balaam through the mouth of the Aſs. Hence, Saint Antony being at Rimini, where there was a great multitude of heretics, deſiring to bring them back to the light of the true faith and to the ways of virtue, for many days did preach and ſet forth to them the faith of Chriſt and of the Holy Scriptures: but they, not only conſenting not to his Holy Words, but even like hardened and obſtinate ſinners refuſing to hearken unto him, Saint Antony one day by Divine Inſpiration went forth to the banks of the river,

cloſe

close beside the sea; and standing thus upon the shore betwixt sea and stream, he began to speak in the guise of a sermon in the Name of God unto the fishes: "Hear the Word of God, ye fishes of the sea and of the stream, since heretics and infidels are loath to listen to it;" and having uttered these words, suddenly there came towards him so great a multitude of fishes, great, small, and middle-sized, as had never been seen in that sea, or in that stream, or of the people round about; and all held their heads up out of the water, and all turned attentively towards the face of Saint Antony, and the greatest peace and meekness and order prevailed: insomuch that next the shore stood the lesser fish, and after them came the middle fish, and still after them, where the water was deepest, stood the larger fish. The fish being thus ranged in order, Saint Antony began solemnly to preach, speaking thus: "My Brothers the fish, you are greatly bounden, so far as in you lies, to thank your Creator that He hath given you so noble an element for your habitation; so that at your pleasure you have fresh waters and salt; and He hath given you many shelters against storm.
He

He hath alſo given you a clear and lucid element, and food, by which you may live. God, your courteous and benign Creator, when He created you, commanded you to grow and multiply, and He gave you His bleſſing: then when the great Flood ſwallowed up the World, and all the other animals were deſtroyed, God preſerved you only without injury or harm. Almoſt hath He given you wings, that you may roam whitherſoever it pleaſes you. To you was it granted, by God's command, to preſerve the prophet Jonah, and after the third day to caſt him up upon the land ſafe and found. You offered tribute to our Lord Jeſus Chriſt, which He, poor and lowly, had not wherewithal to pay. You were the food of the everlaſting King Chriſt Jeſus, before the reſurrection and again after it, by a ſtrange myſtery; for the which things greatly are you bounden to praiſe and bleſs God, Which hath given you ſuch great and ſo many benefits, more than to any other creatures." Upon theſe and other ſimilar words and teachings of Saint Antony the fiſhes began to ope their mouths, and to bow their heads; and by theſe and other ſigns of reverence, according

ing as it was poffible to them, they praifed God. Then Saint Antony, feeing fuch reverence in the fifhes towards God their Creator, rejoicing in fpirit, cried aloud and faid : "Bleffed be the eternal God, fince fifhes of the waters honor Him far more than heretic men, and the unreafoning beafts more readily hearken to His Word than faithlefs men." And as Saint Antony continued his preaching, the multitude of fifhes was increafed yet more, and none departed from the place which he had filled. Upon this miracle the people of the town began to haften forth, and among them were alfo the aforefaid heretics ; the which, feeing fo manifeft and marvellous a miracle, felt their hearts forely pricked, and fell with one accord at Saint Antony's feet, to hear his word. Then Saint Antony began to preach of the Catholic faith ; and fo nobly did he difcourfe, that he converted all thofe heretics and turned them to the true faith of Chrift ; and all the faithful were comforted with great joy, and were confirmed in their faith. And this done, Saint Antony difmiffed the fifhes with the bleffing of God ; and they all departed with marvellous figns of rejoicing,

joicing and likewife the people. And then Saint Antony ftayed in Rimini for many days, preaching, and reaping a fpiritual harveft of fouls.

CHAPTER XLI.

How the Venerable Brother Simon freed from fore Temptation a Brother which for that fame Caufe was about to forfake the Order.

IN the beginning of the Order of Saint Francis, while he yet lived, there came into the Order a young man of Affifi, which was called Brother Simon; the which God adorned and endowed with fo much grace, fuch power of contemplation and elevation of mind, that throughout his life he was ever a mirror of fanctity, according as I have heard from them which long abode with him. But very rarely was he feen outfide his cell, and if ever he did abide with the Brothers, he continually did difcourfe of God. Never had he ftudied the laws of grammar, and neverthelefs difcourfed fo deeply and fo loftily of God and of the love of Jefus Chrift, that his words

words seemed supernatural words; hence one evening he being gone into the wood with Brother James of Maſſa to converſe of God, and ſpeaking moſt ſweetly of the Divine Love, they remained all night in ſuch diſcourſe, and at dawn of day it ſeemed as they had tarried there but a very brief ſpace, according as the ſaid Brother James did tell me. And the ſaid Brother Simon poſſeſſed in ſuch ſuavity and ſweetneſs of ſpirit the divine and loving Light of God, that ofttimes when he did feel it deſcending upon him he would take to his bed; foraſmuch as the tranquil ſuavity of the Holy Ghoſt required of him not alone repoſe of ſoul but likewiſe of body; and in ſuch Divine Viſitations he was ofttimes abſorbed in God, and became wholly inſenſible to all earthly things. Hence, once being thus rapt in God, and inſenſible to the world, the Divine Love burned within him, and he felt naught external with his bodily ſenſes. A Brother deſiring to have proof of this, to ſee if it were even as it ſeemed, went and took a coal of fire and laid it to his bare foot; and Brother Simon knew naught of it, and it made no mark upon his foot, albeit it was held there for a great ſpace

ſpace, until it went out of itſelf. The ſaid Brother Simon when he took his ſeat at table, before ever he partook of bodily food, took for himſelf and did break the ſpiritual food, diſcourſing of God. By his devout converſation he once converted a young man of San Severino, who was in his time a moſt vain and worldly youth, and was of noble blood and very delicate of his body: and Brother Simon, receiving the young man into the Order, retained his ſecular garb in his keeping; and he ſojourned with Brother Simon to be taught of him the meet obſervances. Wherefore the Demon, who labors to diſtort all good, beſet him with ſuch ſore deſire and ardent temptation to ſin, that in no manner could he reſiſt; wherefore he went forth to Brother Simon and ſaid to him: "Give me again my raiment which I wore in the world, foraſmuch as I can no longer ſtand up againſt temptation." And Brother Simon, having much compaſſion for him, ſaid to him, "Sit here, my ſon, a little ſpace with me." And he began to talk with him of God in ſuch manner that every temptation departed from him; and yet again the temptation returned, and he again entreated that his raiment

raiment might be reſtored unto him. And
Brother Simon drove it thence with diſcourſe of God. And this he did many
times; and finally one night the ſaid temptation aſſailed him ſo ſore, more than was
its wont, that being unable by any manner
of means to hold out againſt it, he went
forth to Brother Simon, entreating that his
worldly raiment might be given him again,
for in no manner might he linger longer
there. Then Brother Simon, according as
was his wont, bade him ſit beſide him; and
as he ſpake of God, the young man did lay
his head in Brother Simon's lap, for pure
melancholy and grief. Then Brother Simon,
for the great compaſſion which he had, raiſed
his eyes to Heaven and made a prayer, beſeeching the Lord moſt devoutly for him,
and was rapt and heard of God: hence returning again to his ſenſes, the young man
felt himſelf wholly freed from that temptation, as if he had ne'er felt aught of it: nay
more, the ardor of temptation being converted into the ardor of the Holy Ghoſt,
inaſmuch as he was brought near to the
Living Coal, which is Brother Simon, he
became all inflamed with the love of God
and his fellow-man; inſomuch that, a malefactor

factor being once taken, both whoſe eyes were to be plucked from him, he, that is, Brother Simon, through compaſſion went forth fervently to the Prior; and in full Council, and with many tears and devout prayers, he entreated that from him might be plucked out one eye, and from the malefactor another, to the end that the latter might not be deprived of both. But the Prior and Council, ſeeing the great fervor of the brotherly love of this Friar, did pardon both the one and the other. The ſaid Brother Simon being once at prayer within a wood, and feeling much conſolation in his own ſoul, a band of crows began to confound him with their chatter, at which he commanded them in the name of Jeſus that they ſhould depart and return again no more; and the ſaid birds, departing thence, were thenceforth ſeen no more, neither were they heard either there or in all the region round about. And this miracle was known to all the territory of Fermo, wherein the ſaid Convent ſtood.

CHAPTER XLII.

Of the fair Miracles which God wrought through those holy Brethren, Brother Welcome, Brother Peter of Monticello, and Brother Conrad of Offida: and how Brother Welcome bore a Leper fifteen Miles in most brief Space: and to the one spake Saint Michael, and to the other came the Virgin Mary and laid her Son in his Arms.

THE Province of the Marches of Ancona was of old adorned with holy and exemplary Monks, even as the Heavens are adorned with stars; which same Monks, like unto the luminaries of the sky, did illumine and adorn the Order of Saint Francis and the world by their example and their doctrine. First among these men was Brother Lucius Antico, who was indeed a shining light for sanctity and burned with Divine Charity; whose glorious tongue, informed of the Holy Ghost, gathered wondrous fruit by its preaching. Another was Brother Welcome of San Severino, which was seen by Brother Maximus lift up into the air for a great space, he being at prayer in the wood; for the which miracle the devout

devout Brother Maximus, being then parifh prieft, left his parifh and became a Gray Friar; and was of fuch great fanctity that he wrought many miracles both while he lived and in his death, and his body lies at Murro. The aforefaid Brother Welcome, tarrying once alone at Trave Bonanti, to watch and wait upon a Leper, being commanded of the Prelate to depart thence and go to another Convent which was fifteen miles away, being loath to leave that Leper, with great ardor of brotherly love took him and put him on his back, and bore him from dawn of day even until the rifing of the fun all that fpace of fifteen miles, unto that fame Convent whither he was fent, which was called Mount Sancino; which diftance, had he been an eagle, he could not fo fwiftly have flown in fo brief a fpace: and great were the awe and admiration at this divine miracle throughout all the land. Another was Brother Peter of Monticello, which was feen of Brother Servetus of Urbino (he being then Prior of the ancient Convent of Ancona), raifed up bodily above the earth fome five, ay, fix cubits, even unto the feet of Chrift crucified within the Church before whofe image

image he tarried in prayer. And this Brother Peter, abſtaining once upon the Faſt of the Archangel Saint Michael with much devotion, and being at the laſt of that Faſt in the Church at prayer, was heard by a youthful Friar (who ſtudiouſly remained hidden below the high altar, to ſee ſome act of his ſanctity) diſcourſing with the Archangel Saint Michael; and the words that they ſpake were theſe. Said Saint Michael: "Brother Peter, faithfully you have plagued yourſelf for me, and in divers ways have afflicted your body: lo, I am come to comfort you, to the end that you may require of me whatſoever grace you will, and I will entreat it for you of God." Brother Peter replied: "Moſt Holy Prince and Captain of the Celeſtial Hoſt, and moſt faithful partiſan of Divine Love and pious protector of ſouls, I beſeech you grant me this grace; that you will be pleaſed to entreat of God that He may forgive me all my ſins." Saint Michael made anſwer: "Aſk ſome other grace, for this I moſt cheerfully grant you." And Brother Peter aſked naught elſe ſave only this; and the Archangel concluded: "For the faith and devotion which you have in me, me, I give you this grace which you have aſked, and likewiſe many others." And their converſe ended, which had laſted for a great ſpace, the Archangel Saint Michael departed thence, leaving him exceeding comforted.

In the time of this Holy Brother Peter lived the Holy Brother Conrad of Offida, who, ſojourning together with him in the ſame Convent of Forano in the territory of Ancona, the ſaid Brother Conrad went forth one day into the wood to meditate on God, and Brother Peter went ſecretly after him to ſee what might befall him; and Brother Conrad began to lift up his voice in prayer, to pray moſt devoutly to the Virgin Mary with much piety, that ſhe would obtain for him from her Bleſſed Son this Grace, — that he might feel a little of that ſame bliſs which Saint Simon felt upon the Feaſt of the Purification, when he did bear Jeſus, the Bleſſed Saviour, in his arms. And having prayed thus, the all-merciful Virgin Mary heard his prayer; for lo! the Queen of Heaven appeared to him with her Bleſſed Son in her arms, with exceeding great light; and drawing near unto Brother Conrad, ſhe laid that Bleſſed Babe upon

upon his arm ; and he receiving Him moſt devoutly, embracing and kiſſing Him and preſſing Him to his breaſt, languiſhed quite away, and was conſumed with Divine Love and inexplicable conſolation. And likewiſe Brother Peter, who had ſeen all theſe things from his hiding, felt the moſt extreme bliſs and comfort within his ſoul. And the Virgin Mary departing thence from Brother Conrad, Brother Peter retired in haſte to the Convent leſt he ſhould be ſeen of him ; but after, when Brother Conrad returned again jocund and alert, Brother Peter ſaid to him : " Oh, what heavenly great conſolation was yours this day ! " Brother Conrad ſaid, " What ſayeſt thou, Brother Peter ; and what doſt thou know of that which I have had ? " " Well I know, well I know," ſaid Brother Peter, " how that the Virgin Mary with her Bleſſed Son hath viſited thee." Then Brother Conrad, who being truly humble, deſired to be ſecret with the Graces of God, beſought him that he ſhould ſpeak no word of this to any man ; and ſo great was the love betwixt thoſe twain from that day forth, that they ſeemed to have but one heart and one ſoul between them in all things. And the ſaid Brother

Brother Conrad did once, at the Convent of Siruolo, ſet free a woman who was poſſeſſed of a devil, praying for her all one night and appearing to her mother, at dawn of day did flee thence left he ſhould be ſought out and honored of the people.

CHAPTER XLIII.

How Brother Conrad of Offida did convert a young Monk who afflicted the other Friars. And how the ſaid young Monk, coming to die, did appear to the ſaid Brother Conrad, entreating that he would pray for him: and how he ſet him free by his Prayers from the very great Pains of Purgatory.

THE ſaid Brother Conrad, a wondrous partiſan of Evangelic Poverty and the Rule of Saint Francis, was ſo religious in his life and of ſo great merit towards God, that Chriſt the Bleſſed honored him with many miracles both in his life and in his death; among which upon a time, being come to the Convent of Offida a ſtranger, the Brethren entreated him for the love of God and of true charity to admoniſh a young Monk who did abide in that Convent, the which

which bore himself so childishly, disorderly, and dissolutely that he disturbed both old and young of that Convent, heeding little or naught the divine offices, or other Ordinances of the Rule. Upon which Brother Conrad, through compassion for the young man and at the prayers of the Brothers, did one day call that youth apart; and in a fervor of brotherly love spake to him such efficacious and devout words of admonition, that by the action of Divine Grace he suddenly became, from a child, an old man in his habit, and so obedient and benign and diligent and devout, and moreover so peaceful and so docile, and so studious of all virtuous deeds, that even as before the whole Convent had been disturbed through him, so now all were made comfortable and content through him, and they loved him much. It happened, as it pleased God, that thereafter, after his conversion, the said youth died; at which the said Brothers mourned. And a few days after his death his soul did appear to Brother Conrad, he being devoutly at prayer before the altar of their said Convent, and saluted him piously, as a father; and Brother Conrad asked him: "Who art thou?"

thou?" The same made answer and said: "I am the Soul of that young Monk which did die a brief space since." And Brother Conrad said: "Oh, my most beloved Son, how is it with thee?" The same made answer: "Through the Grace of God and thy doctrines it is well with me, forasmuch as I am not damned: but for certain of my sins, of which I had not time sufficiently to purge me, I must endure the worst pains of Purgatory; thus I beseech thee, Father, as by thy piety thou didst succor me in my living, so now it may please thee to succor me in my torment, reciting certain Paternosters for me; for thy prayers are most acceptable in the sight of God." Then Brother Conrad, consenting kindly to his entreaties, and saying the Paternoster for him but a single time together with the *Requiem æternam*, that Soul cried out: "Oh, beloved Father, what well-being and refreshment I perceive! Now, I beseech thee, say them yet once again." And Brother Conrad did so; and he having recited them, the Soul said: "Holy Father, when thou dost pray for me I feel much ease: hence I entreat thee that thou cease not from worship and praise for me." Then Brother Conrad,

seeing

seeing that that Soul was thus aided by his prayers, recited for him an hundred Paternosters; and when that he had ended them, that Soul did say: "I thank thee, beloved Father, in the name of God, for the brotherly love which thou haft shown towards me; forasmuch as through these thy prayers I am set free from all pains, and am about to enter the kingdom of Heaven." And saying this, that Soul departed thence. Then Brother Conrad, to the end that he might give comfort and joy to the Brethren, recited to them all this Vision in due order. And thus the Soul of that youth entered Paradise through the merits of Brother Conrad.

CHAPTER XLIV.

How the Mother of Christ and Saint John the Evangelist did appear unto Brother Conrad, and did tell him which of they twain did grieve most sore for the Passion of Christ.

IN the days when there abode together in the territory of the Marches of Ancona, at the Convent of Forano, Brother Conrad

Conrad and the aforesaid Brother Peter, which were two shining stars of the Province of the Marches, and two celestially-minded men, forasmuch as between them was so much Love and so much Charity that they seemed but one heart and one soul, they were both bound together by this contract: that every consolation which the Grace of God should grant them they should mutually reveal the one to the other in all brotherly affection. This contract being signed and sealed, it befell that Brother Peter being one day at prayer, and meditating most devoutly upon the Passion of Christ, and how the most Blessed Mother of Christ and John the Evangelist, His most dearly loved Disciple, and Saint Francis, were portrayed at the foot of the Cross, crucified with Christ by mental pangs and dolor, he was seized with a longing to know which of these three did grieve most sore for Christ's Passion,—whether the Mother who bare Him, or the Disciple who had slept upon His bosom, or Saint Francis, which was crucified with Christ; and lingering thus lost in these pious musings, the Virgin Mary appeared unto him with Saint John the Evangelist, and with Saint

Saint Francis, arrayed in moſt fair raiment of beatific glory; but behold! Saint Francis ſeemed clad in more beauteous garb than Saint John. And Peter being all alarmed at this viſion, Saint John comforted him, and ſaid to him: "Fear not, beloved Brother, foraſmuch as we are come to comfort thee in thy doubt. Know, then, that the Mother of Chriſt and I did grieve beyond all other creatures at the Paſſion of Chriſt; but after us, Saint Francis felt greater pangs than any other, and hence doſt thou ſee him clad in ſuch glory." And Brother Peter aſked him: "Moſt holy Apoſtle of Chriſt, why ſeemeth the raiment of Saint Francis more fair than thine?" Saint John made anſwer: "The reaſon is this: foraſmuch as when he lived on earth he did wear raiment more vile than I." And ſaying theſe words, Saint John beſtowed on Brother Peter a glorious garment which he held in his hand, and ſaid to him: "Take this garment, which I have brought to give to thee." And Saint John deſiring to clothe him with this garment, Brother Peter fell to the ground in a maze, and cried aloud: "Brother Conrad, deareſt Brother Conrad, ſuccor me ſtraight; come

come hither and fee marvellous things." And as he fpake thefe holy words that facred vifion vanifhed quite away. Then Brother Conrad coming there, he told him all things in due order as they had happened; and they gave thanks unto God.

CHAPTER XLV.

Of the Converfion and Life and Miracles and Death of that holy Brother, John of the Pen.

BROTHER JOHN OF THE PEN being yet a child and not a churchman, in the Province of the Marches of Ancona, one night there appeared before him a moft beauteous boy, who cried aloud unto him: "John, go forth unto St. Stephen's Church, where there preacheth one of my Gray Friars; believe thou in his teaching, and hearken to his words, forafmuch as I have fent thee thither: and this done, thou muft take a far journey, returning then again to me." Upon which forthwith he rofe up, and felt a marvellous change within his foul; and going forth to St. Stephen's Church, found there a great multitude of men

men and women tarrying to hear the preaching. And he who was to preach there was a certain brother, Brother Philip by name, which was one of the first Friars who had come into the Marches of Ancona; and but few convents had as yet been founded in that region. Going up into the pulpit, this Brother Philip began to preach; and he preached moſt piouſly, not with words of human wiſdom, but by virtue of the Spirit of Chriſt, foretelling the kingdom of Eternal Life. And the ſermon ended, the ſaid child went forth to the ſaid Brother Philip, and ſpake to him: "Father, if it pleaſe thee to receive me into the Order, I will cheerfully do penance, and will ſerve our Lord Jeſus Chriſt." Brother Philip ſeeing and recognizing in the ſaid child a marvellous innocence and a prompt deſire to ſerve God, ſaid to him: "Come to me on ſuch a day at Recanati, and I will ſee that thou art received; for in that place we do intend to make the Provincial Chapter-houſe;" at which the child, which was moſt exceeding ſimple, bethought himſelf that this was the far journey which he muſt take, according unto the revelation which had been made unto him, and thereafter

after he should go thence to Paradise; and so he thought he must do so soon as he had been received into the Order. He went thither, therefore, and was received: and seeing that his thoughts were not then fulfilled, the Head of the Chapter saying that whosoever would go forth through the Province of Provence, through the merit of his holy vow of Obedience, he would cheerfully give him leave so to do, he felt a great desire to go thither, thinking in his heart that even this was the great journey which he was to take before he might reach Paradise; but feeling shame to tell his thoughts, at last he confided them to the aforesaid Brother Philip, who had had him taken into the Order, begging him lovingly that he would entreat for him leave to go into the Province of Provence. Then Brother Philip, seeing his purity and his holy purpose, begged for him this grace: whence Brother John with great rejoicing set about his departure, full of the thought that, his journey ended, he should go thence to Paradise. But, as it pleased God, he sojourned in the said Province twenty-five years in this expectation and desire, living in extreme honesty and sanctity and exemplarity,

plarity, growing ever in virtue and in the Grace of God and of the people, and was supremely loved alike of Monks and laymen. And Brother John being one day devoutly at prayer, and weeping and wailing because his desire was not fulfilled, and that his pilgrimage through this life was too long protracted, there appeared unto him Christ the Blessed, at whose aspect his whole soul was melted within him, and He spake to him thus: "Son, Brother John, require of Me what thou wilt." And he made answer: "My Lord, I know not what other thing to ask of Thee than this, since I desire naught else: but this only do I pray Thee, that Thou wilt forgive me all my sins, and wilt grant me grace to see Thee yet once again, when I may have greater need of Thee." Jesus said: "Thy prayer is granted;" and saying this, He departed thence, and Brother John was left wholly comforted. At the last the Monks of the Marches, hearing the fame of his holiness, spake such great things of him to the Vicar General, that he commanded him by his vow of Obedience to return into the Marches; which command he receiving, set forth joyfully, thinking that, the journey over, he should

should surely rise to Heaven, according to the promise of Christ. But being returned again into the Province of the Marches, he lived there thirty years, and was not known of any of his kindred; and every day he waited for the Mercy of the Lord, that He should fulfil His promise. And in those days he many times filled the office of Prior with much discretion; and Our Lord wrought many miracles through him. And among other gifts which he had of God, he had the spirit of prophecy; hence once, he going forth from the Convent, a certain one among his novices was attacked by a Demon and so sorely tempted that he, consenting unto the temptation, determined within himself to forsake the Order so soon as Brother John should return again from abroad; which thing, both temptation and deliberation, being made known to Brother John through the spirit of prophecy, he straightway returned home, and called before him the said novice, telling him that he desired to hear his confession: but before ever he did confess, he recited to him all his temptation in order, even as God had revealed it to him, and concluded thus: " Son, forasmuch as you awaited my coming,

ing, and would not depart without my bleffing, God hath granted you this grace, that
you fhall never leave this Order, but fhall
die in the Order with the Divine Favor."
Then the faid novice was confirmed in
good-will, and remaining in the Order he
became a holy Monk; and Brother Hugh
told all these things to me. The faid
Brother John, which was a man of bright
and peaceful fpirit, and but rarely fpake,
was a man of great devotion and prayer,
and efpecially after Matins he would never
return into his cell, but would tarry in the
church praying until day. And he being
at prayer one night after Matins, the
Angel of the Lord appeared before him,
faying: "Brother John, the end of your
journey, which you have fo long awaited,
is at hand, and I am come to tell you in
God's name that you may now afk whatfoever favor you will. And I alfo announce
that you may choofe whichfoever you will,
either one day in Purgatory, or a week of
torment in this world." And Brother John,
choofing rather the week of torment in this
world, fuddenly he was afflicted with divers
ills; forafmuch as he was burned with
fever, and pinched hand and foot with
gout

gout, and many other ills; but that which troubled him moſt was, that a Demon ſtood before him and held in his hand a great parchment inſcribed with all the ſins which he had ever ſinned or conceived, and ſaid to him: "For theſe ſins which you have wrought in thought, and with your tongue, and in deed, you are condemned to the loweſt depths of Hell." And he was not mindful of any good thing which he had ever done, neither that he was in the Order, neither that he had ever been; but believed verily that he was damned even as the Demon ſaid. Whence, when he was aſked how he did, he replied :- "Very ill, foraſmuch as I am damned." The Brethren ſeeing this, they ſent for a very ancient Brother, Brother Matthew of Mount Rubbiano by name, which was a holy man and very dear to this Brother John; and the ſaid Brother Matthew, coming to him on the ſeventh day of his tribulation, greeted him, and aſked him how he fared. He made anſwer that he fared but ill, becauſe he was damned. Then ſaid Brother Matthew: "Remember you not that many times you have confeſſed to me and I have abſolved you wholly of all your ſins? and yet

yet again, remember you not that you have ever ſerved God in this Holy Order for theſe many years? and again, remember you not that the merciful kindneſs of God exceedeth all the ſins of the world, and that Chriſt the Bleſſed, our Saviour, hath paid an infinite price for our redemption? And therefore be of good cheer, for verily you are ſaved." And with theſe words, the term of his purgation being fulfilled, the temptation departed from him, and conſolation came. And with great rejoicing Brother John ſpake to Brother Matthew: "Foraſmuch as you are weary and the hour is late, I pray you go to your reſt." And Brother Matthew would not leave him; but yet at laſt, at his great inſtance, he went from him and lay down to reſt: and Brother John remained alone with the Brother who ſerved upon him. And lo! Chriſt the Bleſſed came with exceeding great ſplendor, and with exceſſive ſweet ſmell, according as He had promiſed to appear to him once again when he had greater need of Him; and He healed him of his every ill. Then Brother John with claſped hands gave thanks to God, who with wiſe deſign had thus ended his great journey of the preſent

preſent miſerable life, committed himſelf to the care of Chriſt and rendered up his ſoul to God, paſſing from this mortal life into Eternal Life with Chriſt the Bleſſed, which he had ſo long deſired and waited to ſee. And the ſaid Brother John reſts in the Convent of Brother John of the Pen.

CHAPTER XLVI.

How Brother Peace being at Prayer ſaw the Soul of his Brother, Brother Humility, aſcend to Heaven.

IN the aforeſaid Province of the Marches, after the death of Saint Francis, were two Brothers belonging to the Order; the one was called Brother Humility and the other was called Brother Peace, the which were men of moſt extreme fanctity and perfection; and the one, that is Brother Humility, abode in the Convent of Soffiano, and there did die; and the other dwelt in a community belonging to another Convent quite remote therefrom. As it pleaſed God, Brother Peace being one day at prayer in a ſolitary ſpot was rapt in ecſtaſy, and ſaw

saw the soul of Brother Humility rise straight to Heaven, without any let or hindrance, even in the selfsame moment that it left the body. It then happed that after many years this Brother Peace, who remained, was placed with the Monks of the said Convent of Soffiano, where his brother had died. In those days the Brethren, at the petition of the Lords of Bruforte, exchanged the said Convent for another : wherefore among other things they did translate the relics of certain Holy Friars which had died within those walls : and coming to the sepulchre of Brother Humility, his brother, Brother Peace, took up his bones and washed them with good red wine; and then he wrapped them in a fair white napkin, and with great reverence and devotion kissed them and wept; at which the other Monks marvelled, and held him as an ill example, forasmuch as, he being a man of great sanctity, it seemed that through sensual and secular love he did weep for his brother, and that he showed more devotion towards his remains than towards those of the other Monks, who were no less holy than Brother Humility, and were worthy

worthy of as much reverence as he. And Brother Peace knowing the evil imagination of the Brethren, meekly satisfied them, saying unto them: "My beloved Brothers, marvel not if I do these things to the bones of my Brother and do them not likewise to the others, inasmuch as, blessed be God, I am not led, as you believe, by carnal love; but I have done so because that when my brother passed away from this life I, praying in a desert spot and remote from him, saw his soul rise straight into Heaven; and hence I am assured that his bones are sacred and should rest in Paradise. And had God granted me a similar assurance concerning the other Friars, I should have showed the same reverence to their bones. For the which thing the Brethren, seeing his holy and devout intention, were much edified, and praised God.

CHAPTER XLVII.

Of that Holy Monk to whom the Mother of Chrift appeared when he was infirm, and brought him three Boxes of Electuary.

IN the aforefaid Convent of Soffiano there was of old a Gray Friar of fuch exceeding sanctity and grace that he feemed all divine, and ofttimes was he rapt in God. This Brother being on a certain time quite abforbed in God and exalted, forafmuch as he was notably endowed with the grace of contemplation, there came unto him birds of divers kinds, and familiarly alighted upon his fhoulders, upon his head, and upon his arms, and upon his hands, and marvelloufly did they fing. This man was a folitary foul and but rarely fpake; but when he was queftioned concerning aught, he made anfwer fo gracioufly and fo prudently that he feemed rather an Angel than a man; and he was moft fervent in prayer and contemplation; and the Brothers held him in great reverence. This Brother having fulfilled the courfe of his virtuous life, according to Divine ordinance, he fell ill

ill even unto death, infomuch that naught could he take; and therewithal he would receive no carnal medicine, but all his faith he put in the Heavenly Phyſician, Jeſus Chriſt the Bleſſed, and in His Bleſſed Mother; thereby he merited the divine clemency of being mercifully viſited and healed. Hence he being once in his bed and making ready for death with all his heart, and with all due devotion, there appeared unto him the glorious Virgin Mary, Mother of Chriſt, with an exceeding great multitude of Angels and Holy Virgins, with wondrous ſplendor. She drew nigh unto his bed: whence he gazing upon her was moſt greatly comforted and rejoiced, both in ſoul and in body; and he began to pray humbly that She would pray Her beloved Son that through His merits He would releaſe him from the priſon-houſe of this wretched fleſh. And perſevering in this prayer with many tears, the Virgin Mary replied to him, calling him by name, and ſaying: " Doubt not, ſon, foraſmuch as your prayer is granted, and I am come to comfort you a little before that you depart hence from this life." There were with the Virgin Mary three Holy Virgins, which bore

bore in their hands three boxes of Electuary of matchlefs odor and fweetnefs. Then the glorious Virgin took and opened one of thofe boxes, and all the houfe was filled full of the fmell; and taking a fmall portion of that Electuary in a fpoon, She gave it to the fick man: who, fo foon as he had received it, felt fuch great comfort and eafe that it feemed as his foul could no longer abide within his body; whence he began to fay: "No more, O moft holy and bleffed Virgin Mother! O bleffed Healer and Saviour of mankind, no more! for I am unable to endure fuch fweetness." But the pious and benign Mother ftill offering that Electuary to the fick man and conftraining him to take it, emptied all that box. Then the firft box being emptied, the beatific Virgin took the fecond and laid the fpoon therein to give to him; whereat he did lament, faying: "O moft bleffed Mother of God! my foul is almoft melted away by the ftrength and fweetnefs of the firft Electuary, and how may I endure the fecond? I pray you, bleffed above all Saints and all Angels, that you will be pleafed to give me no more." The glorious Virgin Mary anfwered: "Tafte, my fon, but a little of this fecond ſecond box." And giving him a little, ſhe ſaid : " Now, ſon, you have ſo much as may ſuffice ; be comforted, O ſon, for I will come for you ere long, and will lead you to the kingdom of my Son, which you have ever ſought and deſired." And ſaying this, taking leave of him, She departed thence ; and he was left ſo conſoled and comforted by the ſweetneſs of that confection, that for ſeveral days more he ſurvived ſated and ſtrong, and partaking of no bodily food. And after ſome days, joyouſly diſcourſing with the Brethren, with great jubilee and rejoicing, he paſſed away from this miſerable life.

CHAPTER XLVIII.

How Brother James of Maſſa ſaw in a Viſion all the Gray Friars of the World, after the Faſhion of a Tree, and did know the Virtues and the Merits and the Vices of every one.

BROTHER JAMES OF MASSA, to whom God opened the way to His myſteries, and gave him perfect wiſdom and underſtanding of the Divine Scriptures and of of future things, was of such great sanctity, that Brother Guy of Assisi, and Brother Mark of Montino, and Brother Juniper, and Brother Lucius said of him that they knew no man in the world more familiar with God than this Brother James. Great was my desire to see him; forasmuch as I, praying Brother John, the Companion of the said Brother Guy, that he would expound to me certain spiritual matters, he said to me: "If you would be well informed concerning the life of the Spirit, make shift to have speech with Brother James of Massa:" forasmuch as Brother Guy longed to be informed of him, and no man was able either to add or to take away from his words, not one jot or tittle, and his words are the words of the Holy Ghost, and there is no man on the earth whom I so much desire to see. This Brother James, in the beginning of the ministry of Brother John of Parma, praying was once rapt in God, and remained three days in this state of ecstasy, deprived of all bodily sense, and was so lifeless that the Brethren doubted whether he were not dead; and in this trance God revealed to him the future of our Order: for the which thing, when I heard

heard it, my defire to hear him and to fpeak with him did but wax ever greater. And when it pleafed God that I fhould have occafion to talk with him, I befought him thus: "If thofe things be true which I have heard of thee, I prythee keep them not hidden from me. I have heard that when thou didft lie three days as one dead, among other things which God revealed unto thee was that which was to befall this our Order; and this was I told by Brother Matthew, preacher in the Marches, to whom thou didft reveal it in compliance with thy vows of Obedience." Then Brother James with great humility acknowledged that the words of Brother Matthew were true. His words, that is, thofe of Brother Matthew, the preacher in the Marches, were thefe: "I know, Brother, unto whom God hath made known that which fhall befall our Order, forafmuch as Brother James of Maffa hath publifhed and told me, that after many things which God revealed to him concerning the future ftate of the Church Militant, he faw in a vifion a beauteous and very great tree, whofe roots were made of gold, the fruits which hung upon its boughs were men, and they all were

Gray

Gray Friars, the chief branches being divided according to the number of the Provinces of the Order; and upon each branch hung ſo many Friars as there were in the Province appropriated to that branch; and thus he knew the number of all the Friars in the Order, and of each Province, and alſo their names and ages and conditions, and the great offices and dignities and eſpecial graces belonging to each, and their offences. And he ſaw Brother John of Parma at the higheſt tip of the midmoſt bough of this tree; and in the topmoſt twigs of the branches, which grew about this midmoſt branch, ſtood the miniſters of every Province. And after this he ſaw Chriſt ſeated upon a great white throne; and Chriſt called Saint Francis to ſit beſide him, and gave him a Chalice full of the Water of Life, and ſent him forth, ſaying: 'Go, viſit your Brethren, and give them to drink of this Cup of the Water of Life; foraſmuch as the ſpirit of Satan ſhall riſe up againſt them and ſhall daſh them down, and many among them ſhall fall and ſhall not riſe again.' And Chriſt gave to Saint Francis two Angels which ſhould walk beſide him. And then came Saint Francis to offer the Cup

Cup of Life to his Brethren: and he did firſt offer it to Brother John of Parma, who, taking, drank it all, every drop, devoutly and in haſte; and ſuddenly he became luminous as the ſun. And after him ſucceſſively Saint Francis offered it to all the reſt: and there were but few among them who with due reverence and devotion did take and drink it all. They who took it piouſly and drank it all, every drop, ſtraightway became ſplendid as the ſun; and they which ſpilled it on the ground and received it not with meet piety, became black, or dark and miſſhapen, and horrible to look upon: they that drank a part and poured out a part became partly luminous and partly ſhadowed, and in greater or leſs degree, according to the meaſure of that that they drank and ſquandered; but more than all the reſt the aforeſaid Brother John ſhone reſplendent, which moſt complacently had drank the Cup of Life, whereby he had moſt deeply contemplated the abyſs of infinite light, and therein had perceived the adverſity and tempeſt which were to ariſe againſt the ſaid tree, to ſhake and agitate its branches. Wherefore the ſaid Brother John departed from the tip of the bough

bough whereon he stood, and descending downwards through all the boughs, did hide himself amid the great limbs of the tree close to the trunk, and there abode in pensive mood: and a certain Brother, which had taken a portion of the Cup and had squandered a part, mounted up to that branch and that twig whence Brother John did descend. And being on the said twig, the nails of his hands were changed to sharp and piercing steel, like unto razors: upon which he did move from that place whither he had climbed, and with force and fury would fain have thrown himself upon the said Brother John to do him an injury; but Brother John seeing this, cried out in a loud voice, and confided himself to the care of Christ, which sat upon the throne; and Christ at his call summoned Saint Francis, and gave him a sharp flint stone, and said to him: 'Go with this stone and cut the nails of yonder Friar, with which he would fain claw Brother John, to the end that he may do no manner of harm to any man.' Then Saint Francis came and did even as Christ did command him. And this done, there came a whirlwind, and shook the tree so sore that the Brothers fell to earth; and

and the firſt to fall were they who had ſpilled all the Cup of the Water of Life, and were borne thence by Demons to realms of darkneſs and torment. But Brother John, together with the others which had drunk all the Cup, were tranſlated of Angels to the abode of Life and Eternal Light and of Beatific Splendor. And the aforeſaid Brother James, who ſaw the viſion, underſtood and knew particularly and diſtinctly that which he ſaw, reading clearly the names and conditions and ſtates of each. And ſo long endured that tempeſt about the tree, that it fell, and the wind bore it away. And then ſo ſoon as the tempeſt did ceaſe to rage, from the root of that tree, which was of gold, ſprang forth another tree, which was all of gold, which brought forth flowers and fruits and foliage of gold. Of the which tree, and of its increaſe, ſize, beauty, odor, and virtues, it is better to be ſilent than to ſpeak at this preſent."

CHAPTER XLIX.

How Chriſt appeared to Brother John of Vernia.

AMONG the other wife and holy Brothers and ſons of Saint Francis, who, as Solomon ſaith, are the glory of their father, there lived in our times, and in the ſaid Province of the Marches, the venerable and holy Brother John of Fermo, the which, by reaſon of the great ſpace that he abode in the Holy Convent of Vernia, and for that he there paſſed away out of this life, was alſo called Brother John of Vernia, foraſmuch as he was a man of rare life and of great ſanctity. This Brother John, being a layman and yet a child, deſired with all his heart to follow the way of true repentance, which ſhould keep his ſoul and body clean and pure; hence, being but a little lad, he began to bear about him a breaſtplate and an iron belt next his ſkin, and to keep great faſts, and eſpecially when he ſojourned with the Canons of Saint Peter of Fermo; which lived ſplendidly, he would ſhun ſenſual delights, and mortify his fleſh with moſt rigid faſtings.

faſtings. But his companions being moſt contrary to him in this, tearing from him his breaſtplate and hindering him in divers faſhions from faſting, he, inſpired of God, bethought him to forſake the world and its lovers, and to caſt himſelf wholly into the arms of Chriſt crucified, with the habit of the crucified Saint Francis; and even ſo he did. And being received into the Order thus young, and committed to the care of the Maſter of the Novices, he became ſo ſpiritual and devout, that once on a time hearing the ſaid Maſter diſcourſe of God, his heart melted within him like wax before the fire; and with ſuch exceeding ſweet grace was he warmed by Divine Love, that he, not able ſteadfaſtly to endure ſuch great ſuavity, roſe up, and, like a man drunk in ſpirit, ran hither and thither, now through the garden, now the wood, and now the church, according as the flame and fury of the ſpirit did urge him on. Then in the courſe of time Divine Grace did make this angelic man to grow from virtue to virtue, and in celeſtial gifts and divine exaltation and ecſtaſies, inſomuch that at certain times his mind was exalted to the ſplendors of the Cherubim, at other times

to

to the joys of the Bleſſed, and yet again to the loving and extraordinary embrace of Chriſt. And eſpecially upon a certain day was the flame of Divine Love once kindled in his heart, and this fire burned within him for the ſpace of three years, in which time he received marvellous conſolations and Divine viſitations and was ofttimes rapt in God; and did speedily appear all on fire and aflame with the love of Chriſt: and this was on the holy Mount of Vernia. But inaſmuch as God is ſtrangely watchful of his children, giving them, according to their various neceſſities, now conſolation, now tribulation, now proſperity, and now adverſity, according as He ſees it needful to uphold them in the way of humility, or the more to enkindle their deſire after celeſtial things, it pleaſed the Divine Bounty, after the three years, to take away from the ſaid Brother John that bright beam and that flame of Divine Love, and to deprive him of all ſpiritual conſolation. For the which Brother John was left without light and without the love of God, and was quite comfortleſs and afflicted and ſad; wherefore he wandered through the wood, roaming hither and yon, calling with groans

groans and tears and sighs to the beloved Spouse of his soul, which had hidden Himself and departed from him, and without whose presence his soul could find no rest neither any repose: but in no place, neither in any manner, could he meet his sweet Jesus, or again recover those most dear and divine delights of the love of Christ, which had been his wont. And this tribulation endured for many days; during which he persevered in continual weeping and sighing, and in praying God that of His pity He would restore to him the beloved Spouse of his soul. At the last, when it pleased God to have sufficiently proved his patience and inflamed his desire, one day, as Brother John walked in the said wood thus troubled and afflicted, he sat down to rest in sheer languor, leaning against a beech-tree, with his face all bathed in tears, gazing Heavenward, and lo! suddenly there appeared Jesus Christ close beside him in the very path by which Brother John came thither, but saying naught. Brother John seeing Him and knowing Him well, that He was Christ, suddenly threw himself at His feet and with inordinate tears most humbly besought Him, saying:

saying: "Help me, Lord, for without Thee, my sweetest Saviour, I live in darkness and in the midst of tears; without Thee, most meek and gentle Lamb, I live in anguish, in pain and fear; without Thee, Son of God Most High, I live in confusion and shame; without Thee I am stripped of every good, and blind, forasmuch as Thou art Christ Jesus, True Light of souls; without Thee I am lost and damned, forasmuch as Thou art the Spiritual Life, and the very Life of Life; without Thee I am withered and dry, forasmuch as Thou art the Fountain of every gift and every grace; without Thee I am all comfortless, forasmuch as Thou art Jesus, our redemption, love, and desire, the Bread that doth comfort, and the Vine that maketh to rejoice the hearts of Angels and the hearts of all the Saints. Shine upon me, most gracious Master and most loving Shepherd, forasmuch as I am Thy lamb, unworthy though I am." But to the end that the desire of holy men, unto which our Lord is slow to hearken, might be kindled unto greater love and merit, Christ the Blessed departed thence and left him unheard, neither spake He any word, and went His way along that self-same

same path. Then Brother John rose up, and hastened after him, and yet again did fall at His feet, and with a holy importunity did hold Him by His garment, and with most pious tears besought Him, saying: "O sweetest Jesus Christ, have mercy upon my tribulation; hearken unto me for the abundance of Thy mercy, and for the truth of Thy salvation, and give me back the light of Thy countenance and of Thy loving kindness, forasmuch as the whole earth is full of Thy merciful deeds." And Christ departed from him yet again, and spake not to him, neither gave He him any consolation; and He did even as the mother doth to her child, when she lets him long for her breast, and lures him to pursue her with weeping, to the end that so he may take it more gladly. At which Brother John once more with greater fervor and desire followed after Christ; and having drawn nigh to Him, Christ the Blessed turned to him, and looked upon him with a gracious and smiling countenance; and opening His most holy and merciful arms, He did most sweetly embrace him. And in that opening of His arms Brother John saw rays of resplendent light to issue from the

the moſt Sacred Breaſt of the Saviour, the which lighted all the wood and pierced his very ſoul and body. Then Brother John knelt at Chriſt's feet; and the Bleſſed Jeſus, even as He did to Magdalen, gave him His foot to kiſs. And Brother John, taking it with ſupreme reverence, bathed it in ſo many tears that verily he ſeemed another Magdalen; and he cried devoutly: "I pray Thee, O Lord, that Thou wilt not regard my ſins, but by Thy moſt Holy Paſſion, and by the ſhedding of Thy moſt Precious and Holy Blood, that Thou wilt revive my ſoul by the grace of Thy Love; ſince this is Thy command, that we love Thee with all our hearts and with all our minds; which command can none fulfil without Thy aid. Aid me, then, moſt beloved Son of God, for I love Thee with my whole heart and my whole ſtrength." And Brother John, entreating thus at Chriſt's feet, was heard of Him, and again received from Him his former grace, which is the flame of Divine love, and felt himſelf quite conſoled and renewed; and knowing the gift of Divine grace to have returned into him, he began to give thanks unto Chriſt the Bleſſed, and devoutly to kiſs His feet. And then riſing up

up to gaze upon the face of Chrift, Jefus
Chrift ftretched forth and offered him His
moft Sacred Hands to kifs: and when that
Brother John had kiffed them, he drew
near and fell upon Chrift's bofom and embraced and kiffed Him ; and Jefus likewife
did embrace and kifs him. And in thefe
kiffes and embraces Brother John enjoyed
fuch Divine odors, that had all the odorifer-
ous delights and all the perfumed things of
earth been conjoined together, they would
have feemed but an evil ftench in compari-
fon with that fmell; and therein Brother
John was rapt and confoled and enlightened, and that fmell dwelt in his foul for
many months. And thenceforth, from his
mouth, which had drank of the Fountain of
Divine Wifdom in the Sacred Bofom of the
Saviour, came forth marvellous and celeftial
words, which turned all hearts; and they
that heard him reaped much fpiritual harveft: and in the path in the wood wherein
had ftrayed the Bleffed Feet of Chrift, and
for a good fpace round about, Brother John
did ever fmell that fmell, and fee that fplendor, whenfoever he returned thither for a
great time thereafter. Brother John returning again to himfelf after that ecftafy,
and

and the bodily prefence of Chrift being vanifhed, he remained fo enlightened in foul, in the depth of his divinity, that albeit he was no fcholar by human ftudy, neverthelefs he did miraculoufly folve and expound the moft fubtle and profound queftions concerning the Divine Trinity and the deep myfteries of the Holy Scriptures. And many times thereafter, fpeaking before the Pope and his Cardinals, and before the King and his Nobles, and the Doctors and learned Men of the Law, he put them all in great amaze by the wife decrees and lofty words which he did utter.

CHAPTER L.

How, faying Mafs upon All Souls' Day, Brother John of Vernia faw many Souls fet free from Purgatory.

THE faid Brother John, once faying Mafs upon All Souls' Day, for all the fouls of them that are dead, according as the Church hath decreed, offered up that moft noble Sacrament with fuch lovingkindnefs and fuch pious compaffion that for its

its efficacy the fouls of the dead defired above any other good that he might be chofen of all men to fay fervice for them; for he feemed to melt quite away in the fweetnefs of his pity and brotherly love. For the which thing, as he did devoutly raife aloft the Body of Chrift in that Mafs, offering it unto God the Father, and praying Him that for love of His Bleffed Son Jefus Chrift, Which hung upon the Crofs to buy back fouls, He would be pleafed to fet free from the pains of Purgatory the fouls of the dead, created and redeemed by Him, ftraightway he faw an almoft infinite number of fouls' rife up out of Purgatory, as they had been countlefs fparks of fire flying up from a burning furnace; and he faw them go up into Heaven, through the merits of Chrift's Paffion, which is every day offered up for the quick and the dead in that moft Sacred Hoft, worthy to be adored in *fæcula fæculorum*.

CHAPTER LI.

Of the Holy Brother James of Fallerone; and how, before he died, he did appear to Brother John of Vernia.

AT the time when Brother James of Fallerone, a man of much sanctity, lay very ill at the Convent of Moliano in the territory of Fermo, Brother John of Vernia, who was then abiding at the Convent of Maſſa, hearing of his affliction, foraſmuch as he loved him like his own dear father, fell to praying for him, devoutly entreating God in ſilent prayer that He would make whole the body of the ſaid Brother James, if it were for his ſoul's beſt good ; and praying thus devoutly, he was rapt in ecſtaſy, and ſaw in mid-air a vaſt army of Angels and Saints above his cell, which was in the wood, encompaſſed with ſuch ſplendor that all the region round about was lighted up with the glory thereof ; and among theſe Angels he ſaw the ſick Brother James, for whom he prayed, arrayed in white and ſhining robes. He alſo ſaw among them the bleſſed
Father

Father Saint Francis, adorned with the Sacred Stigmata of Chriſt, and of exceeding luſtre. He alſo ſaw and recognized Holy Brother Lucius, and Brother Matthew the Prior of Mount Rubiano, and many more Friars, the which he had never ſeen nor known in this life. And Brother John gazing thus with great delight, as was his wont, upon that bleſſed band of Saints, there was revealed to him as a verity the Spiritual Salvation of the ſaid ſick Brother, and that he muſt needs die of his diſeaſe; but he ſhould not go ſtraight to Paradiſe after death, inaſmuch as it beſeemed him firſt to purge his ſins a little ſpace in Purgatory. At the which revelation Brother John did ſo greatly rejoice for that ſoul's ſalvation that he heeded not the death of the body, but with great ſweetneſs of ſpirit called him ſoftly, ſaying: " Brother James, my dear father; Brother James, my dear brother; Brother James, moſt faithful ſervant and friend of God; Brother James, Companion of Angels and Conſort of the Bleſſed." And thus in this aſſurance and cheer he returned again to himſelf, and incontinently did ſet forth from the Convent and go to viſit the ſaid Brother James

at

at Moliano; and finding him so heavily burdened that he could scarce speak, he announced to him the death of his body and the glory and salvation of his soul, according to the assurance which he had received through Divine revelation; at which Brother James, much rejoiced in soul and in aspect, received him with great cheer and with a jocund laugh, thanking him for the good tidings he did bring, and devoutly recommending himself to his prayers. Then Brother John besought him dear, that after his death he would return and speak to him concerning his condition; and Brother James gave him his promise so to do, if it should thus please God. And having said these words, the hour of his passing away drew near, and Brother James began piously to recite that verse of the Psalms: *In pace in idipsum dormiam, et requiescam;* which is to say: I will lay me down in peace, and take my rest; and having repeated this verse, with a light and jocund face he passed away from this life. And after that he was buried, Brother John travelled thence to the Convent of Massa, and awaited the promise of Brother James that he would return again to him
upon

upon the day which he had named. But on the ſaid day, he being at prayer, Chriſt did appear unto him with a great company of Angels and of Saints, among whom Brother James was not; whence Brother John, marvelling much, recommended him fervently to Chriſt. Then the day following thereafter, Brother John praying in the wood, Brother James did appear to him accompanied by the Angels, all glorious and all bright, and Brother John ſaid to him: "O deareſt father, why did you not return again unto me upon the day which you did name?" Brother James replied: "Foraſmuch as I had need of certain purgation; but in that ſame hour that Chriſt appeared to you, and you did commend me to His care, Chriſt heard you and delivered me out of all puniſhment. And then I appeared unto Brother James of Maſſa, a lay ſaint, which was ſerving at Maſs, and ſaw the Conſecrated Wafer, when the Prieſt did raiſe it up, converted and changed into the form of a moſt beauteous living boy, and ſaid to him: 'I go this day with this ſame child unto the realm of Eternal Life, whence can none go without him.'" And ſaying theſe words, Brother James diſappeared,

peared, and rofe up to Heaven with all that bleffed company of Angels; and Brother John was left greatly comforted. The faid Brother James of Fallerone died upon the eve of the day of Saint James the Apoftle, in the month of July, at the aforefaid Convent of Moliano; wherein for his merits the Divine Bounty wrought many miracles after his death.

CHAPTER LII.

Of the Vifion of Brother John of Vernia, wherein he knew the whole Order of the Holy Trinity.

THE aforefaid Brother John of Vernia, forafmuch as he had perfectly abjured every mundane and temporal comfort and delight, and had put all his pleafure and all his hope in God, Divine Bounty gave him wondrous confolations and revelations, efpecially at the high feafts of Chrift; whence the folemn feaft of Chrift's Nativity once drawing nigh, whereon he furely awaited comfort from God in the fweet humanity of Jefus, the Holy Ghoft poured
into

into his foul such great and excessive love and longing for the brotherly affection of Christ, through the which He did abase Himself to take on our humanity, that verily it seemed as his soul had been dragged from his body and were burning like to a furnace. Unable to endure which ardor, he grieved and melted apace, and cried out in a loud voice, forasmuch as through the force of the Holy Ghost, and through the overmuch fervor of his love, he could not longer restrain his cries. And in that same hour when that measureless fervor came upon him, with it came so strong and sure a hope of his salvation, that he could not in any manner believe that if he were dead he must needs pass through the pains of Purgatory; and this love endured in him full six months, albeit that excessive fervor was not continual, but came upon him at certain hours of the day. And at this time he did receive marvellous visitations and consolations of God: and ofttimes was he rapt, as he was seen of that Brother which first wrote down these things; among which, he was one night so mightily exalted and rapt in God that he saw in Him the Creator of all created things both celestial and terrestrial,

terrestrial, and all their perfections and degrees and various orders. And then he knew clearly how every created thing looketh in the eye of its Creator, and how Our Lord is above, and within, and without, and beneath all created things. He also saw and knew one God in three Persons, and three Persons in one God, and the infinite loving-kindness which did make the Son of God incarnate through obedience to the Father. And lastly and finally, he knew in that vision how that there is no other way by which the Soul can journey to God and have Eternal Life, save only through Christ the Blessed, which is the Way and the Truth and the Life of the Soul.

CHAPTER LIII.

How, saying Mass, Brother John of Vernia fell as one Dead.

TO the said Brother John, as he did abide in the aforesaid Convent of Moliano, there did hap on a certain time this wondrous chance, as those Brethren which were present do relate; for the first sennight

sennight after the feast of Saint Lorenzo, and during the sennight of the Assumption of Our Lady, he having said Matins in Church with the other Friars, and the unction of Divine Grace coming unlooked for upon him, he went forth into the garden to meditate upon Christ's Passion and to prepare himself to celebrate with all due piety the Mass which it was his duty that morning to sing; and pondering the words of the consecration of the Body of Christ, that is, considering the infinite Compassion of Christ, which led Him to redeem mankind, not only with His most Precious Blood, but also to leave with us His most Worthy Body and Blood as food for our hungry souls, his love of the sweet Jesus began to wax within him in such fervor and such suavity that his soul could no longer endure such piercing sweetness; but he cried aloud, and as one drunk in spirit ceased not from saying, *Hoc est corpus meum:* forasmuch as saying these words he seemed to see the Blessed Christ with the Virgin Mary and a multitude of Angels, and as he said these words he was enlightened of the Holy Ghost concerning all the deep and lofty mysteries of that most high Sacrament.

ment. And at day dawn he entered the Church with that fervent fpirit and with that felfsame anxious pang, and repeated ever thofe fame words, thinking himfelf heard of none and feen of none; but a certain Monk knelt in the choir at prayer, which heard and faw all. And unable in that ardor to reftrain himfelf, through the abundance of Divine Grace, he cried out in a loud voice, and fo long he did continue thus, that it was the hour to fay the Mafs; wherefore he went to trim the altar; and beginning Mafs, the farther he proceeded fo much the more grew his love of Chrift and that fervor of devotion with which he was given a fenfe of the ineffable God fuch as he himfelf knew not, nor could exprefs it after with his tongue. Wherefore he, fearing left that fervor and fenfe of God fhould wax fo great that he muft need leave the Mafs unfaid, was greatly troubled, and knew not which part to choofe; whether to proceed with the Mafs, or to ftay and await what might befall. But forafmuch as another time a fimilar chance befell him, and the Lord had fo tempered that ardor that he was not forced to leave the Mafs unfaid, and trufting that fo he might have

have ftrength to endure again, he went on and finifhed the Mafs with great fear; and coming even fo far as the Preface of Our Lady, the Divine Illumination and Gracious Suavity of the love of God began fo to grow upon him, that, reaching the *Qui pridie*, he could fcarce endure fuch excefs of fuavity and fweetnefs. Finally, attaining unto the act of confecration, and faying one half the words over the Hoft, that is, *Hoc eft*, in no manner could he go farther, but ftill did repeat thofe felfsame words, that is, *Hoc eft enim:* and the caufe why he could not proceed farther was, that he felt and faw the prefence of Chrift with a multitude of Angels, whofe majefty he could not fuffer, and he faw that Chrift would not enter into the Hoft, or rather that the Hoft could not be tranfubftantiated into the Body of Chrift, unlefs he did utter the other half of the words, that is, *corpus meum*. At the which he, lingering thus in anguifh, and not proceeding farther, the Prior and the other Monks, and even many laymen which were in the Church to hear the Mafs, haftened towards the altar; and they ftood affrighted as they faw and confidered the acts of Brother John, and many among them wept for pure piety.

At

At laſt after a great ſpace, that is, when it pleaſed God, Brother John uttered the words, *enim corpus meum*, in a loud voice; and ſuddenly the form of the Wafer vaniſhed, and Jeſus Chriſt the Bleſſed appeared within the Hoſt incarnate and glorified, and ſet forth unto him the humility and charity which did incarnate Him of the Virgin Mary, and which daily maketh Him to deſcend into the hands of the Prieſt when he doth confecrate the Hoſt; whereby he was the more exalted in ſweetneſs of contemplation. Hence, having lifted up the Hoſt and confecrated Cup, he was rapt out of himſelf; and his ſoul having loſt all ſenſual and fleſhly ſenſe, his body did fall backwards; and if that the Prior had not held him in his arms as he ſtood behind him, he would have fallen to the ground. At which the Brethren drawing nigh, together with thoſe laymen which were in the Church, both men and women, he was borne away thence into the ſacriſty like unto one dead, foraſmuch as his body was quite cold, and the fingers of his hands were clenched ſo cloſe that they had much ado to ſpread or move them. And in this manner he did lie as one ſenſeleſs, or rather

rather rapt, even until Tierce, and ſo remained. And foraſmuch as I, who was preſent at theſe things, deſired mightily to know thoſe things which God had wrought in him, ſtraightway that he did return to himſelf I did go in to him, and did pray him for the love of God that he would tell me all. Hence he, becauſe he had great faith in me, did narrate to me all in order: and among other things which he told me, he declared that as he conſidered the Body and Blood of Chriſt Jeſus which were before him, his heart was liquefied like unto well-tempered wax, and it ſeemed as his fleſh were deprived of bones, in ſuch manner that he could not lift either hand or arm to make the ſign of the Croſs above the Chalice. So, too, he told me that before ever he became a Prieſt it was revealed to him of God that he ſhould but ſeldom go to Maſs; but inaſmuch as he had already ſaid many Maſſes, and this thing had never yet befallen him, he bethought himſelf that the revelation came not from God. And nevertheleſs ſome fifty days before the Aſſumption of Our Lady, whereon the aforeſaid chance befell him, he did receive yet another revelation of God, telling him that

that this chance fhould befall him on
about the faid feaft of the Affumptio[n]
but he remembered not thereafter the f[ore]
vifion, or rather revelation, made to h[im]
by Our Lord.

www.ingramcontent.com/pod-product-compliance
Lightning Source LLC
Chambersburg PA
CBHW020804230426
43666CB00007B/847